COC

COOKING COCKROACH

Joey Truman

Whisk(e)y Tit

NYC & VT

In some instances, the author has recreated events, locales and conversations from recollection. In order to maintain anonymity, identifying details may have changed. But mostly not. Joey is Joey. George is George. The Publisher is the Publisher. Jonny is Jonny. Tina is Professor Curly. Generally speaking, though, this is a work of creative memoir, and should not be used in any indemnifying or otherwise inhumane manner.

Cover design: Murphey Wilkins
Book design: Miette Gillette
Cover photo: Tina Satter
Cover art and drawings: Joey Truman

If you are inspired to use any or all parts of this book in your own project, have a little class and tell us how you wish to use it: miette@whiskeytit.com.

Copyright ©2018 by the author.
ISBN 978-1-7329596-0-6

To Peg-Leg, you are a good mom, Mom.

CONTENTS

Prologue	ix
The Tender Bean	1
Campfire Chicken Leg	5
Saltine Crackers with American Cheese Slices	11
Four Dollar Three Day Hot Pot	17
Tex-Mex Tacos	25
Theoretical Steaks	33
The Dishwasher's Dilemma	41
Part Two of The Dishwasher's Dilemma	47
Hot Dogs	55
Notes On A Couple Spices	63
The Taco Burger	71
Filing For Chapter 11	79
A Recipe For Disaster	85
Bacon	91
Gravity Juice From A Vertical Meat [Seven Dollar Bank Taco]	97
The Ten Dollar Week	105
Feelings	113

Chunk Rib With Garlic Foist	119
The Remainders	129
Freezer Soup	137
The Paycheck	147
One More For The Road	151
About the Author	156
About the Publisher	157
Acknowledgements	158

PROLOGUE

Everybody likes food. It's tasty. You die if you don't eat it. It smells good, and looks good. If you eat too much, you get fat. If you eat too little, you get skinny. These are facts. When I was 17, I almost starved to death, then again at the age of 31, then again at the age of 37.

I only know I almost died from reading accounts of dire adventures, by recognizing the signs: lethargy, apathy, the inability to get out of bed. Stealing food and hoarding food.

But starving to death is no excuse for a lousy meal.

Some of the best meals are on an empty stomach. The rich use aperitifs to create this effect; the poor, circumstance. One of the best meals in my life I was living in Laramie, Wyoming. I had dropped out of school and was trying to make a rock band happen. None of us had jobs. I was already skinny and was getting skinnier. I had trouble getting out of bed. I had many dreams. Mostly about a huge ball in the middle of my room that was made of wax. I kept trying to add slices of wax to it. One day my friend Jacob, the drummer, came into the room and handed me a piece of pizza. The pizza was moist and hot and crusty. It had pepperoni and green peppers. Delicious! Soon after eating it I was able to get up and go into the kitchen. I was hoping for more. They, my friends and bandmates, were eating the pizza. Turns out I was the guinea pig. They had found the pizza in a dumpster behind a pizza place downtown. I didn't care. They gave me another slice. The second was just as good as the first!

This was the beginning. I didn't cook this meal, of course, but I did experience its transcendent flavors and delivery. Not long after this my brother moved in and started playing bass for the band. He was older. Had a desire to become a chef. He taught me the basics. How to boil water. How to treat eggs. A simple tortilla recipe that translates to all breadstuffs, like using cigarette ash for leavening. I took it all in.

Years later a roommate would refer to me as a cockroach that could cook. I took it as a compliment.

The recipes here are simple but efficient. They require nothing more than a fire and a pan and a desire to stay alive.

Bon appétit!

THE TENDER BEAN

Beans are easy. They are very cheap. You can buy them dry in bags, but they are better in cans. Two reasons: they require no soaking and they are sterile. The best beans are black beans. Kidney beans are chunky and dry. Garbanzo beans are gross. Pinto beans are rough on the system.

Black Beans In Water

Ingredients

Can of black beans
Salt [teaspoon]
Water [quarter can]

Tools

Pan
Spoon

Method

Take a can of black beans and open it. Pour it in the pan. Put water in the can to 1/4 of the way up. Stir the water. Pour the water in the pan. Put the can next to the stove and put the spoon in the can. Turn the heat to high. Bring the beans to a boil. Add salt. Reduce to a simmer. Wait.

Stir the beans. After a while the water will start to coagulate. When this happens, taste the beans. Add more salt if needed.

This process takes longer than expected, but the beans will need attention the whole time, they tend to stick to the bottom of the pan. You will know that the beans are done when they are no longer chalky and the sauce is thick enough that it coats the spoon in a way that you need to use your teeth to remove it.*

*Note: If at any point during this process the beans get too thick, just add water and start the process again.

CAMPFIRE CHICKEN LEG

Ingredients

Cooked chicken leg [skin removed]
Olive oil
Butter
Salt
Pepper

Tools

Campfire
Grill
Daughter
Peanut gallery

Method

When I was a teenager my mom would buy fried chicken from the grocery store deli counter. It always made me sick to eat it. I don't know if it was because it was undercooked or just because it was sitting around all day, but unless I microwaved it before I ate it I would obtain a low-grade nausea. To this day chicken makes me queasy. This recipe takes this into account.

First, go camping with somebody that cooks a bunch of chicken legs the night before and removes all the skin. Whether they remove the skin before cooking, or they just eat it is up for debate and remains an unknown.

Next, get up early the next day to find it raining. This is important because you will want to spend a long time building a fire that uses wet logs that have been thrown in the bushes from two years ago that were even then deemed too wet to burn. You will want to spend some time getting chastised by a friend about using the dry wood to make this wood burn. Don't listen to him. He is an asshole.

Next, take a hatchet and cut chunks of rotting, dryish wood from a fallen tree a little deeper in the bushes, preferably walking over used toilet paper and empty beer cans to get there.

Next, bring the chunks of rotting, dryish wood to the fire pit and stack in a way that they make the fire very smoky. Observe people moving to get out of the smoke. Feel bad.

Finally, and this is critical, do this for hours, three at least. While doing this make a marinade of onions and garlic and salt and cider for the carnitas that you mistakenly thought was going to be for lunch, but is intended for dinner.

Now your fire should be ready for cooking.

During this time people will get hungry. They

will make turkey sandwiches with cheese and mayonnaise. Kids will run around and shoot homemade bows and arrows. It should continue to rain.

The Dish

First, your friend who cooked the chicken leg the night before will offer you one. Initially you will say no, but then you will decide you are hungry. Go with him to the car and get it. He will make a joke about how it is in the trunk like he is selling bootleg DVDs. Laugh at his joke and ask him about whether he will be offended if you heat up the chicken leg. Look him in the eye. He will say no.

Next, flip the grill on top of the coals you have made. The grill will be connected to the metal fire pit ring and will be hard to adjust. Smoke will get in your eyes and people will ask what you are doing. Ignore this and watch as the grill heats up. When enough time has passed, put the chicken leg on the grill. It should sizzle and stick to the grates.

Next, notice that the chicken is sticking to the grill. There is no fat because there is no skin. Turn the chicken leg hoping for different results. Things will in fact remain the same.

Next, remember there was some butter on one of the picnic tables that you saw earlier. Remove the chicken leg from the grill and go looking for the butter. You won't find it. This will frustrate you, but you will remember that there was some olive oil in the cooler. Put the chicken leg on a paper plate one of the kids had been using for macaroni and cheese. This will add some zest. Go to the cooler and find the olive oil. Drizzle it on the chicken leg. Add copious amounts of salt and pepper. Roll it around on the plate. Take the chicken leg back to the grill and place it. At this point the grill should be very hot. The chicken leg should sizzle.

Next, cook the chicken leg. The peanut gallery will give you guff, ignore this, they have nothing better to do because it is still raining, and most of them have started drinking at this point.

Next, move to the side because the fire is smoky again. Your daughter should be sitting next to you at this point. She will be holding a stick and wanting to whittle. Her knife will be in her tent and she won't be able to reach it without taking off her shoes and she wants you to go get it. You can tell her to wait 1 [one] second while you flip the chicken leg over. When she asks you again, go to the tent she and her mother are sleeping in. Take the chicken leg with you. It will be delicious.

Next, eat the chicken leg as you are helping your daughter get her knife. The outside meat will be hot, but the interior will be cold. Make a note of this and stop eating. Go back to the fire and put the mostly eaten chicken leg on the grill. You will have the same problem as before with the chicken sticking to the grill. Take the chicken leg back to the picnic table and notice the butter showed up again.

Chicken and cheese go hand in hand. It makes perfect sense that butter and chicken would do the same. This assumption is correct. This is how you finish the dish.

To Finish

Roll the remaining chicken leg on the plate with the salt and pepper and olive oil. Add more salt and pepper to taste. Take the chicken leg back to the grill and place it on top. The fire will be colder now, but don't worry, slower cooking is now better.

Next, go cut a hank of butter from the stick. A tablespoon at least. Place it on top of the chicken leg, near the top, where most of the meat remains. Watch it melt slowly while the peanut gallery heckles you. Ignore this. They will be jealous when you are finished.

Finally, when the butter has melted the chicken leg is done. Eat it. It will be buttery and salty and peppery. Throw the bone back on top of the grill and wait for the rain to stop. You will be heckled more, but when the sun comes out you will be left alone with only the memories of a tasty treat dangling from your taste buds and the satisfaction of a job well done.

SALTINE CRACKERS WITH AMERICAN CHEESE

SALTINE CRACKERS WITH AMERICAN CHEESE SLICES

I grew up in Wyoming. Poor. The middle child of five boys. My father was a carpenter. My mother ran a day care out of the house called Grandma's Rocker. During the school year we were taken care of by the system, but in the summer we became irritating. Meaning, my mom would kick us out of the house right after breakfast and we weren't allowed to return until dinnertime when all the kids had been picked up from the day care.

My brothers and me. We all had bikes and we lived on the edge of town. The edge of town meaning farmland, meaning sugar-beet fields and the canal. The canal led to Slick Creek, pronounced: Slick Crick.

We were allowed to ride our bikes on the dirt roads through the fields and along the canal, but we weren't allowed to play in the ditches with the irrigation pipes or in the canal. The canal became a playground in the winter, only when it was empty and useless.

Slick Crick. The canal went through a flume

over it. The land on either side was public. Teenagers did graffiti on the flume and smoked cigarettes. Mostly at night. The pipe itself was probably 6 ft [six feet] in diameter and 60 ft [sixty feet] long. There were endless debates about what would happen if you jumped in at the entrance. Whether or not you could hold your breath to the other side. Rumors. Kids that had done it.

This is where we would ride our bikes in the morning. There were two swimming holes. A climbing cliff made out of dirt that was impossible to climb. A spooky section of wilderness that supposedly some teenage Satanists hung a cat in. From a tree.

The morning would usually go like this:

Depending on who was sleeping on the floor—we only had one bed between me and my two younger brothers, so we had to rotate, two in the bed, the other on the floor—he would wake up first and wake up the other two. Breakfast of pancakes and bacon. The other two brothers would show up to breakfast later. They had their own beds and shared a room, they could sleep longer. Also, their room had a door.

Next, our dad would leave and go to work.

Not long after this, day care kids would start to get dropped off. Our mom would start yelling at us to get lost. The house would begin to fill with toddlers. Her employee would always be late. And if she managed to be on time she was worse than our mom about yelling at us to get lost. Usually a wooden spoon was involved.

This next recipe is simple, but transitory. Best served to a person on the go.

Ingredients

2 [two] sleeves of saltine crackers [hopefully name brand]
American cheese slices in cellophane, 6 [six] slices [adjusted for crackers, 4 crackers equals 1 slice]
Pair of binoculars
Backpack

Tools

Bikes
Summer

Preparation

Your binoculars will probably be already in the backpack, so as you are being chased down the hallway with the wooden spoon you won't need to worry about them. Just grab the bag and go.

Method

Run back through the kitchen and out the side door of your house. Nobody will be chasing you at this point because you will have already worn them out. Have your brother throw the cheese and crackers in the bag. Zip it up. Put it on. Get on your bike. Ride to Slick Crick with your brothers and the friends you pick up on the way.

Next, ditch your bikes by the flume. Hide them just in case. This is always a good practice.

Don't get caught, even if you aren't doing anything wrong.

Next, spend the morning exploring and swimming. You will be wearing shorts and get sunburned, don't worry, this is natural. Use the binoculars to see a farmhand work the irrigation pipes far away. Then see a bird. Hand them over. He won't see the bird. Discard.

Next, it will be past noon and everybody will be so hungry that they can't take it anymore. Find some shade down by the creek. It will be muddy, but there won't be mosquitoes. Sit down and take inventory.

The Dish

2 sleeves of crackers and 6 packs of American cheese in cellophane.

Remove the red wire pincer from the crackers. Discard.

Remove the cheese from the cellophane.

There will be 7 [seven] of you, 5 [five] brothers and 2 [two] friends. This means you will need to divide the cheese in a way that you can all share. I would suggest splitting them into fifths or ninths, that way it won't be obvious who got the short stick.

Distribute the crackers and cheese.

The crackers should be sweet and salty with a bit of crunch. The cheese should almost coat the tongue without interfering with the ubiquitous notion of sustenance.

You will be hot, and your skin will feel dry and burned.

Follow this meal with a long romp in a dirty section of muddy water that will allow your parents to force you to take a bath when you get home.

FOUR DOLLAR THREE DAY HOT POT

More often then not when you are starving you will find yourself with limited funds. Having less than five dollars tends to be the point of panic, in my experience. It is this moment when you have to choose between smoking, $3.50 for a package of Top Tobacco; drinking, $1.50 for a Coors Tall Boy; and eating.

At a distance this choice should be clear; you eat, but it is not that simple. The body is far more resilient than the mind. Almost autonomous. There is a point when starving that you become incredibly sharp and focused. Your body vibrates with the universe. You almost don't want to eat, just to see how far you can push it. Death is no longer abstract. This is the reason some cultures use starvation as a tool to get in touch with nature.

The dark side to this, however, is society. Society views the destitute as delinquent. The poor are poor because they are stupid. If you weren't stupid you wouldn't be poor. This is hard knowledge when you are on the receiving end, but the logic is almost certainly sound:

Why would you choose cigarettes or beer over food?

The answer is quite simple: because being alive is not about staying alive. To be hungry is one thing, to be miserable, another. There is this notion that if you work hard enough for long enough you will be successful. This may be true, but it does not take into account the fact that life itself is a material thing, a machine, that all parts, the mind included, need maintenance.

I recently read about a conversation between a reporter and a war veteran who was living under a bridge. The reporter wanted to know if the veteran was a reliable witness to the transaction that he had seen [a congressman talking to an informant.] The veteran was most likely suffering PTSD [post-traumatic stress disorder]. He was homeless for a reason. He couldn't adjust back to society. The reporter said:

"Were you drunk?" [when you saw this]

"You think I sleep under the bridge sober?"

Starving is hard. Sometimes you need a break. Cigarettes suppress hunger and give you a distraction. Booze helps you not think. Choices are not always choices. There have been times in my life when I would much rather have a cigarette than a slice of pizza. Other times, the opposite.

There are moments when the balance is almost equal. You have five dollars to your name. A place to live. Money, coming to you soon, you just need to last a few days. A bag of smokes in your pocket and a couple beers in the fridge.

This next recipe will get you through the next three days, with little to no discomfort.

Ingredients

Can of black beans, $.99
1 pound of chicken backs, $.98
1 can of peeled tomatoes, $1.19 on sale
1 bag of corn tortillas, $1.29
Total: $4.45
Salt and pepper [if around]

Tools

Large pot
Spoon or fork
Bowl for eating

Method

Put medium flame under pot, if you have butter or oil of any kind, add now.

Allow the pot to heat up, if you have butter or oil wait for the butter to turn brown, or the oil to begin to shimmer, if not, just wait until the pot seems really hot and add chicken backs skin side down.

If you have butter the skin will start to fry. If you have oil there will be a flame, remove the pot from the fire and wait until it cools down enough to put back on the fire. If you don't have butter or oil there will be smoke. Remove the pot and run water over the chicken backs. They will start to boil. You will have wanted to fry them, but that is not an option anymore. Let them simmer.

As the chicken backs fry/simmer remove the lids from the canned beans and canned tomatoes.

The chicken backs will be ready to turn over. Take the spoon/fork and flip them. Add salt if you have it. Pepper too, if you have it.

At this point you will want to taste the chicken back because you are hungry. It will be hot and burn your fingers. Leave it alone.

The chicken back will begin to bleed through the bones. This will be the sign that you should add the can of tomatoes and can of beans. Fill one of the cans with water and add to the pot. Stir. Bring to a boil. Reduce the heat to a simmer.

Simmer slowly.

The tomatoes will start to break apart. You will grow impatient and start to mash them with your spoon/fork. This is ok. Roll a smoke. If you have a beer, open it. Smoke the cigarette with your spoon/fork in your hand, tasting the sauce frequently. Wish you had an onion and garlic.

When the sauce reduces down 1/4 of the way you won't be able to help yourself. Take a corn tortilla from the package and heat it up on a burner. Heat one side until it starts to sag, flip it over. Heat until it bubbles. Place in hand. It will be almost too hot to handle. Take your spoon/fork and dig out some beans and chicken back. Put on top of the tortilla burning your hand. Roll upon itself. Eat.

This will be unsatisfying. The dish will not be done yet, but the food in your belly will give you patience.

Finish your cigarette and beer.

Wait.

Twenty minutes should go by before you try to eat it again. The sauce should thicken and should have dark flavorful spots where the heat bubbles out. Taste sauce often. Smoke and pace.

The Dish

Heat tortilla.

While heating tortilla, spoon/fork as much of the bean and tomato and chicken back into a bowl as possible.

Dip heated tortilla in sauce as you are eating the bean/tomato/chicken back.

Repeat.

The simple nature of this dish is almost angry. It will almost always be consumed alone and in a state of panic. The chicken backs in the beginning are separate from the beans and tomato sauce. As time goes by this dish starts to take on a mush-like quality that is unpleasant, therefore enjoy the first few bowls while you can.

However, this dish can be left on top of the stove

for as many days as it takes to eat it. Just heat it up whenever you are hungry.

If lucky, you can throw it in the trash before you are done with it. Because you have money for other meals. Then you can just feel guilty for wasting food instead of hungry and terrified.

TEX-MEX TACOS

TEX-MEX TACOS

My first job was a dishwasher. My second job was a dishwasher. My third job was a telemarketer. My fourth job was a dishwasher. My fifth job was a ticket-man. My sixth job was a nude model. My seventh job was a deli-man. My eighth job was a dishwasher. My ninth job was a carpenter. My tenth job was a drywaller. My eleventh job was a dishwasher. My twelfth job was a taco-maker. My thirteenth job was a taco-maker.

Being a taco-maker is a good job. It combines all the other jobs into one tasty asylum. I never got sick of being a taco-maker. The pay was terrible, which is the only reason I quit it. You can't live on taco-maker wages. Unless you are in college. Unless you have roommates galore. I was both and had both.

College was funny. I dropped out of high school on my 17th birthday and hitchhiked to Laramie, Wyoming. Started a band. Starved for a while. Moved to Powell, Wyoming. Briefly. Then moved to Denver, Colorado. Kept starving. Moved to New York City, starved some more, went on tour, moved back to Wyoming and then decided to go to college. I got a job as a drywaller in the summer and taught myself trigonometry. I wanted to be a physics major. I needed to get into the advanced math classes. I had to test in. I also needed to get my GED [General Education Diploma].

I got my GED. I also tested in. But because I was poor, I had to get a job to supplement my income. I had Pell grants, which means what, I don't know. Poor Entreaty for Listless Losers? The Food-Stamps of College Credit. AKA [also known as], another way to make poor people feel unwelcome. But you don't have to pay those grants back. So fuck you too.

I was poor. I got a job. The job was at a taco place.

The job was pretty funny. I had to be there early. 9 a.m. Which is early when you are young. The first thing I had to do was cook the meat. The meat came in big tubes. Ten-pound tubes. There was a large cauldron. You turned it on and sliced the beef in half. Ground beef. You squeezed everything out. Then you threw the plastic bag in the trash. You did this again. Then you cooked the beef until it was browned. Twenty pounds of ground beef.

The next step was to add the secret mix of spices and hardener. It was mostly cumin and baking soda, I think. It also has an addener, or a plus one, that makes the beef larger. A plumper of sorts. Like beef, but filler.

At this point you take the water-sprayer and

hose the beef down. This boils the cooked beef and makes it even. This is good because it makes your job easier later. You stir it and let it boil. There are timers that you push when you are doing this. They tell you everything.

When the beef is done you dump it into pans that will be placed at the front of the line. There will be three. Two will go on the line and one will go into the fridge for the lunch rush. The steam tables will change the beef from a sloppy mess to a codified cement-like structure. You will cover this and make the beans.

The beans are in a bag. Dump them into a pan. Add water. Put the pan in the steam table.

By now it is 10 a.m., and you are wondering why you are there so early. The lunch rush doesn't start until 11:30. The manager is an asshole is why. He tells you to go and clean the lobby. When you are done he says you need to sweep the drive-through. The first order is bunk because the night shift already should have done it, but those jerks are a bunch of stoners and forgot, or more likely, they knew you would have to do it anyway, so … but sweeping the drive-through is okay because you can smoke.

With a smoke hanging from your mouth you sweep the drive-through. Your shirt smells. You didn't notice it inside because it smells like the inside. But now it smells. It smelled before. The face you make is angry. You sweep cigarette butts from the gutter. You wonder who was throwing cigarette butts on the ground. You throw a cigarette butt on the ground. You stamp it out. You sweep it up.

Five minutes go by. You wish it was more. But you were wrong and it's already 11:30. The drive-through. The first car. You make your way back inside. You hear it: A number 3. Two soft shells and a Potato Ole. Doctor Pepper.

You wash your hands. The tortilla press is hot. You drop an order of Ole's in the fryer. You press two torts. Before you know it the order is out the window. A tasty meal, out the window. They asked for super hot sauce, a tiny cup of ground pickled jalapeños.

The lunch rush begins.

The lunch rush is nice. Two hours of zero thinking. Action. Fry this. Wrap that. Squirt this. Squirt that. Bags of food and chaos. Then it is over. A job well done. Soak the pans if you are on dish duty. Clean the lobby if you are on lobby duty. Sweep the drive-through if you are drive-through duty. This is the best duty, because you can smoke. A coveted enterprise.

Ingredients

1 pound of ground beef
1 hunk of cheddar cheese
1 head of iceberg lettuce
1 taco kit* [hard]

* Note: While I find it imprudent to make popular culture references while dealing with such timeless notions such as starvation, I will mention that the Taco Bell Hard Taco Kit is far superior to the Old El Paso or Ortega taco kits. Although, the Old El Paso Taco Kit has a far better taco sauce. However, the spice packet is not nearly as good, and the taco shells tend to come broken, which is a deal-breaker to me.

Method

In a skillet, brown ground beef. Add salt and pepper if you have it. Next, open the taco kit box. Take the seasoning from the box and set it next to the stove, on the counter. Take the sauce packet and if you have scissors cut a triangle from the corner. Try and make the opening as small as possible, the packet is unwieldy and tends to make a mess if not properly opened.

Next, remove the plastic from the lettuce. Take the top two leaves from the head and whack the stem on the counter. This will allow you to remove it without spreading salmonella. Throw the stem and the outer leaves in the trash. Take whatever knife you have and cut a chunk off. Cut the chunk into smaller chunks.

Next, open the cheese. If you have a cheese grater use it. If not, cut really small pieces of cheese. Cold cheese is the easiest to cut and grate. If the kitchen is hot throw the cheese in the freezer to cool it down.

Next, when the meat is browned cut the top of the seasoning open. Scissors work best. [For some reason, the seasoning packets can't be ripped open.] Pour the seasoning on top of the meat. Fill the empty seasoning packet with water. Pour it on top of the meat. Stir.

The seasoned meat will boil and start to solidify. When the water evaporates turn the heat off. You will know this has happened because the liquid in the skillet becomes pure oil. Let the meat rest and open the package of hard corn tortillas. Be careful not to break them. They are delicate.

The Dish

Take a tortilla shell from the bottom of the stack. Hold it in your hand and put some meat in it. Place cheese on top of the meat. Squirt some sauce on top of the cheese. Add lettuce. Eat it while standing at the stove. Over the skillet. Do this six more times until you are full. Your roommates will more than likely come to kitchen while you are making this. They will want a taco. Resist this because you are still mad about the toilet seat incident. [Yeah, I was sitting on it when it broke, but one of you is obese and the other one takes 7 [seven] shits a day. I think we should all pitch in to buy a new seat. And! How does somebody use a toilet seat wrong? That is nonsense, Jakers!]

Nature

You will fall asleep after this meal. You will wake up to find that your roommates have eaten the rest of the tacos. It will make you sad, but what can you do? Tasty tacos are delicious.

THEORETICAL STEAKS

THEORETICAL STEAKS

When I was 18 I was living in Denver [Colorado]. My friend Mike had a two-bedroom apartment on High street that me, Jacob, Rocky, Larae, Marty, Alexis, and Keith moved into. Jacob, Rocky, Marty, and I had a band. It was called Uwe. I sang. Jacob played drums. Rocky, bass. And Marty, guitar. The apartment had one mattress that Mike slept on. He had his own room. The mattress was on the floor. The other bedroom is where the rest of us slept. I remember having a sleeping bag and using dirty clothes as a pillow. There was a couch in the living room, but nobody slept on it because you could never get any sleep.

Somehow we all got jobs at the Ticketmaster Call Center downtown. The job was simple but horribly depressing. Minimum wage, which was $5.50 at the time. And at the end of every phone call you had to explain the service charges and processing fees. Meaning, on top of the overpriced ticket you were charged an extra $10 to $15 just for the privilege of giving your money to Ticketmaster. Every single phone call made you feel gross. Which, on an average day, you did about 10 calls an hour, times 8 hours a day. Which meant you felt gross 80 times a day, at least.

There were two shifts. The day shift, which was from 8 a.m. until 4 p.m. And the night shift, which was from 4 p.m. until midnight. I worked the day shift for some reason. I think it was because I could get a break from all my roommates. I guess. In retrospect it seems insane to get up so early during those times, but I do remember being annoyed surrounded by so many people all the time. So that is why.

The best way to get to work was to take the Number 15 bus down Colfax. Well, when you could afford it. It cost 90 cents. I didn't take it often for this reason, but when I did I always noticed this guy staring at me. This is where this recipe comes from.

One day in particular, summer, I was taking the bus downtown to get my paycheck. If I remember correctly it was for $207.53 for two weeks of work. My day was planned out accordingly:

- Take bus to work.
- Get check.
- Take check to check cashing place.
- Cash check.
- Treat myself to a hot dog.

This didn't happen. What happened instead was:

I got on the bus. The Number 15 going down Colfax. The old man that liked to look at me was on the bus. At the time I was 18. A translucent punk rocker wearing a suit jacket and knickers with blue striped socks. My hair was dyed black. I am sure I was wearing makeup. Painted fingernails. Point being, it didn't occur to me that he was looking at me more than just an average old guy checking out a weirdo. His look was different than normal though. Decided. He had a cane, so I took him at face value. He was just an old guy staring at me.

I got off the bus when it stopped on Broadway. I walk fast, so I was surprised when I heard a clanking gate behind me moving faster than I was. I stopped and turned around. The old man from the bus was walking as fast as he could. He held up his hand, out of breath and said:

"Hey, wait, hold on!" I stood there a little confused before becoming completely confused. Social interactions tend to hypnotize me. I can watch myself acting, but I can't do anything to stop or change my reaction. It is very frustrating. I am like a fainting goat.

"Yeah?"

"Hi, I'm Daniel." He held out his hand, catching his breath.

"Joey," I said, shaking his clammy hand.

"What are you doing? You're a model, right?" I was flattered. I did feel like a model. I was 18 and on my own. I had all sorts of glorious plans for my future.

"I'm not a model, no. Just going up here to get my check, I guess." I would have told him my life story had he not interrupted me.

"You want to be a model?"

"Maybe, yeah, I suppose."

"I'm a photographer." Daniel took his wallet out. He handed me a card. It said: Daniel Angelo; Photographer. I looked at it. He held his hand out for me to give it back. I gave it back. "Get your check, I'll wait."

***

The building where I worked was on the corner of Broadway and Colfax. The woman that sold the hot dogs I planned on eating as a treat parked her cart next to the escalators that went inside. I was hopeful for those hot dogs. I took the escalator up. I didn't want to talk to Daniel anymore. But the idea of being a model intrigued me. Easy money for being good looking. I got my check and folded it in half. I put it in my pocket. I poked around for a while killing time. Maybe if I took too long Daniel wouldn't be there anymore. He was. I watched him watch me as I took the escalator back down.

He smiled at me when I got to the sidewalk. I looked at the hot dog woman with a sense of remorse. This guy was really goosing my plan. But, I don't know. I think I was excited. He said:

"Come on, I'll buy you a coffee."

He took me across the street and bought me a coffee. It was a fast food joint, that even in my destitution I avoided. He made chit-chat about the decor for long enough that I was about to stand up and walk out. He realized this and said:

"Ok, let me cut to the chase. You're a real good-looking dude, I want to take some pictures of you. I don't have any money, but I can feed you steaks."

The thought of steaks made me hungry. I wanted a steak. At this point I knew he was up to no good, but the thought of eating something proper made my mind crack. I said:

"Oh, yeah?"

"Yeah, I got a bunch of guys, and we just take photos and hang out. Come on, you done with your coffee? My place is just down the street. I'll show you."

***

Daniel took me to his building. There was a placard on the front of the building that said: Grove Forest Assisted Living. It was an old-folks home. I should have walked away. I didn't.

We took the elevator to his floor. The building itself was dank and smelly. There wasn't a single thing that said yes. I did though. He brought me into his apartment. The place was disgusting. He had a long-haired cat that shed. His walls were covered in terrible framed photographs he had taken of naked men in the forest. He had me sit on the couch. His shedding cat rubbing against my legs and trying to get on my lap. He poked around in his stack of photos hoping to find the photo to really put me in the mood. It was a black man with a huge boner standing next to a tree. Daniel said:

"I kept sucking him off, but he wouldn't get soft. It was so frustrating. I use Vaseline to get this effect. What do you think? What do you think about this?" He unzipped his pants and took out his penis. I stood up at this point and ran out the door. I took the stairs down. When I got to the corner I could hear him calling my name. He had to take the elevator. In my mind he was shaking his cane at me. Come back. I stopped taking the bus.

Ingredients

A tasty steak in the mind.

Process

Allow yourself to be vulnerable and preyed upon.

Conclusion

Don't be poor.

Garnish

The taste of this dish will last you for the rest of your life. Write a hit play about it.

THE DISHWASHERS DILEMA

THE DISHWASHER'S DILEMMA

My first paying job was as a dishwasher at a restaurant/bar called The Office Bar and Lounge. I was 15. I got the job because my mom was a waitress there. I worked Friday and Saturday nights. The two busiest nights of the week. On Friday night they had a rotating special. Sometimes steak. Sometimes cabbage burgers. Sometimes a dish that one of the cooks came up with. Usually with noodles. Or a special burger. Like a Blue Burger, which was a hamburger with blue cheese and bacon.

Saturday nights the special was always prime rib.

I made five dollars an hour. I worked from 6 p.m. until the kitchen closed and I finished my duties, which was around 11:30 p.m. It was a simple job. It went like this:

- Show up on time. Always on time. There is never an excuse. Both my parents taught me this. My dad specifically though, mainly because his teaching usually had a hint of anger underneath that seemed threatening. My mom was more practical and made it seem like a good practice. Which is probably why it took me until my 35th year of being alive to realize that it is in fact a load of horse shit. Nobody expects you to be on time. If you are on time, people will only exploit you. It makes you look weak. Because you look weak, people take advantage. Don't show up on time. Not to work, not to parties, not to lunch, not to interviews, not to haircuts, even airplanes. If you are the last person to show up to a plane about to take off, running down the jetway, screaming "Wait!" as they are closing the doors. Every time, every single time, they will put you in first class. Because dealing with one $1,000 person in the front of the plane is much easier than dealing with ten $100 assholes in the back [I am partially joking about this. I do believe my lack of success has much to do with not being an asshole at all times, but my philosophy is that you shouldn't be an asshole. Ever. It makes the world suck. But if you want to be successful, be an asshole. To everybody. At all times. You will be taken seriously. Human nature.]

- Wash the potatoes. The Office had very dirty potatoes. They were quality potatoes, but I think they came straight from the field. You had to scrub them with a green pad. Not only that, but they had to soak for a while. And Michael, the owner of the establishment wouldn't let you use warm water because hot water was limited. The work was cold and harsh. You had to use the sinks in the kitchen to do it. There were three of them. Which meant you had to fight with the cooks in the kitchen the whole time because they always needed two, one clean and one dirty, one for produce and one for the flash-pans, which was their way of cleaning skillets with out washing them. Heat them until they smoke, dip them in the water.

- Organize the potatoes. Put the clean potatoes in a 5-gallon bucket. Fifty of them. Fill another bucket half full with cold water. Drain the sink. Take both buckets out of the kitchen and heave a sigh of relief.

- Make fries. In the hallway between the kitchen and the pantry there was an apparatus that turned potatoes into square strips that could be deep-fried. It had a lever and knife grid. The knife grid was very hard to clean. The square strips ended up in the bucket that was half-filled with water. This prevented them from browning. The water. The job was enjoyable. Every time.

- Take the bucket of fries into the walk-in cooler and cut the steaks. Michael liked the way I cut the steaks. I had a good eye. There were always two slabs of deboned beef rib in the cooler that needed cutting. I enjoyed doing this, but it always made me nervous. I don't think I ever failed. Or if I did, I had to eat the steak, which was not at all a form of punishment.

- Wash the dishes that have been piling up. By this time the place was packed. People were yelling at each other. The grill was covered in steaks. The fryers were bubbling with fries.

I think I need to come back to this because it isn't as simple as it seems.

Process

Hold your horses.

Idiom

Always a bridle's-maid, never a horse in the mouth.

PART TWO OF THE DISHWASHER'S DILEMMA

Why was the dishwasher taken off the football field? Because he had a [dish]-located shoulder.

Why did the dishwasher need so many quarters? Because he needed to make a long [dish]-tance phone call.

Why was the very boring and flamboyant man like a steak? Because he was a flambé-ing yawn [filet mignon].

The only person below the dishwasher in the kitchen hierarchy is the busboy. But this in and of itself is nebulous. Often the dishwasher is the busboy as well. There was one job in particular I had where I was the dishwasher, the busboy, and the janitor. That one was rough. Specifically the women's bathroom. FYI, the hover method doesn't work with explosive diarrhea. At least put the seat up first. Somebody does, and will, have to clean up after you.

But back to the beginning

My job started with scrubbing potatoes in the busy kitchen. Old women farting on me. The water cold, so Michael could save a few pennies. The potatoes caked with dirt, so Michael could save a few pennies. In the end, a 5-gallon bucket of clean potatoes. Take those potatoes to the pantry. Find an empty 5-gallon bucket. Put it on top of the overturned 5-gallon bucket under the french-fry slicer. The french-fry slicer was a grid of thin metal blades about the size of a square drink coaster. This was connected to the bottom of a lever that was attached to two pistons that were attached to another solid metal grid that had nubs that fit precisely into the slots of the slicer itself, the foister. This entire apparatus was attached to the wall. As annoying as these details are to write, and likely to read, I mention them to make a point.

There was an art to making fries

First, to make the fries, you had to lift the lever, hold the potato on top of the slicer, bring the lever down until the foister met with the potato, remove your hand, press through.

If the potato wasn't centered properly you ended up with mashed chunks of off-cuts that gummed up the machine.

If the potato was too big for the slicer you ended up with mashed chunks of off-cuts that gummed up the machine.

If the machine was gummed up you had to spend precious minutes cleaning the slicer, which was annoying. The machine was brutish but delicate. A gummed machine meant you couldn't go all the way through, which meant you were stuck with a potato head in the slicer itself, which you would have to dig out with a steak knife.

While you are doing this, the kitchen is getting busier. The old women farting on you. Yelling for things from the pantry. You can hear the waitresses putting dishes in your sink in the dish room. And fuck, the slicer is gummed.

It doesn't matter. You finish the job. You lug the 5-gallon bucket of fries back into the kitchen and fill it with water to keep the potatoes from turning color. Now it is twice as heavy but you manage to lift it out of the sink and lug it to the walk-in cooler. You can see all the dishes backed up in your sink on the way. Suddenly you are sweating as you open the cooler door. You put the bucket next to the two others that were there from when the pantry cook came on.

There is a moment of peace when the door shuts behind you. Surrounded by tubs of mayonnaise and produce. You cut 10 steaks from the slab of beef sitting on a baking pan. You put the knife down. You wipe the blood from your fingers on your apron.

You open the door to mayhem. The kitchen is

insane. The country band has started playing covers of modern songs you can't stand. The waitresses are suddenly screaming for salads. It is busy enough that this is now your job. You go back into the walk-in cooler and get two with blue cheese and a ranch. You put croutons on and put them on the station.

The station is a series of shelves by the entrance to the kitchen. It is a manifold. Where the bar meets the kitchen meets the hallway meets the walk-in meets the dish room.

The next hour is salads. Thousand Island. Blue cheese. Ranch. Lite ranch. Oil and vinegar. There are tubs of iceberg lettuce with shredded carrots in the walk-in cooler. Cold clear glass plates. Dinner salads.

But the dishes in your sink, ignored.

But suddenly they are out of steak plates and soup cups. Time to shine.

Run to the kitchen and clean the sinks. Run hot as possible with soap in the first one. Cold with a pellet of oxide in the second. Leave the third open for the cooks. Run back to the dish room and scrape. Scrape and stack. Scrape and stack. Rinse and stack. Rinse and stack. Transfer. Transfer.

Suddenly you are back in the kitchen getting farted on. Now with yelling. Joey! Soup cups. Joey! Bread boards. Joey! Blue and ranch, no croutons! Fries! Out of knifes! Where the hell is that ice cream! Break table 3!

Suddenly you are out on the floor breaking table 3. Your middle school math teacher is saying:

"Hi Joey, working hard, or hardly working?" She is holding a Long Island Iced Tea.

"Hi, Mrs. Hammond." You break the table so she can sit down. You can tell she is drunk.

"Got any plans for the summer?"

"I guess work, I guess." You blush and fumble. Sweat drips down your nose. You wipe the table with a rag that smells like bleach and run away.

Back in the dish room you scrape and stack. The silverware is overdue so you dump the water out of the bucket it has been soaking in and take it to the kitchen. You dump it into the wash sink when someone yells we are out of fries. You go to the walk-in and get a bucket of fries. You carry it between your legs because it is heavy. You replace the bucket next to the fryer. This bucket is lighter. You take it back to the dish room and dump it out. The left over fries clog the sink. As you are dealing with this there is a loud clicking noise. Someone yells:

"Pepsi's out!"

You go back into the walk-in cooler and switch the bag in the box. The sound goes away.

Someone yells:

"We need silverware!"

You run back into the kitchen and do the silverware. Your hands are bright red at this point. But the night seems to be letting off. You run back to the dish room and scrape plates. Your trash is full, so you take it out of the bin and tie it off. You take it to the back door. You leave it. You go back to the dish room and scrape and rinse dishes.

The night tapers off.
Suddenly it stops.
The kitchen is closed.

The next hour is spent scraping and stacking dishes. Taking them to the kitchen to be washed. Washing dishes and silverware. Pots. Pans. Taking out trash. Cleaning the slicer and the foister. Taking up the mats in the kitchen. Sweeping and mopping.

I guess I will end this the way I started, the dishwashers dilemma:

What to eat after your shift?

The Office Bar and Lounge had the very best prime rib, but the thing about access:

"Show me the easiest life in this world, and I will show you somebody who is bored with it."

The Meal

Fried Chicken Sandwich With Peppers, Mayonnaise, And Spicy Cheese

The Method

Michael had a special ability with both bread and mayonnaise. As long as you caught her before she shut the fryer down you would never be displeased.

The Sandwich

Two slices of Michael's bread
One piece of fried chicken from the distributor, probably Swann's
One piece of spicy cheese
Spicy mayonnaise that Michael made

The Method

Put it on the station and take a bite every time you walked by it.

In Addition

Sometimes the waitresses put money in your pocket afterward for helping them out.

HOT DOGS

Hot dogs are a simple food. They come in all sorts of flavors and sizes. They can be spicy or bland. Meaty or tofu. They can be long and chewy or short and greasy. Sometimes they bend, sometimes they are straight arrows. They are easy to digest. Easy to cook. They take condiments in stride the way sex takes foreplay, meaning better. They almost can't be ruined. Here is a list of things you can put on a hot dog:

Mayo
Mustard
Jalapeños
Ketchup
Cheese
Onions
Pickles
Chili
Sauerkraut

But also

Mayo: Spicy mayo, Miracle Whip, Lame hippie mayo, Asian mayo (Jonny's mayo)
Mustard: Yellow mustard, German mustard, Chunky mustard, Grey Poupon
Jalapeños: Fresh jalapeños, Pickled jalapeños
Ketchup: Brand Name, Catsup, Packet Ketchup In A Drawer Left Over From Take-Out
Cheese: American, Nacho, Cheddar
Onions: Raw, Cooked

In Norway, they wrap hot dogs in bacon and fry them. In Germany, they eat them with a tiny little bun that you hold between your index finger and your thumb. In Mexico, they call them chorizo and make tacos with them. In America, they come in packages of ten while the buns you eat them with come in packages of eight. I think Big Bread is behind this disparity, but let's not talk politics.

When I was starving to death in Laramie, Wyoming, my brother Buck came home one time with a package of hot dogs and buns. He also had an onion and some jalapenos. I remember this well because the way he cooked the hot dogs was simple; he boiled them, but what he did while cooking them changed the way I thought about food.

He chopped the onion and the jalapeno into small little chunks. I guess they call this a dice. I mean, I know this is a dice, but at the time I did not, but it was also closer to a mince, but it wasn't that either. He put the dice/mince in a bowl and added vinegar [which I think was left over from the people that had lived there before], mustard [which came from packets], sugar [also packets], and salt and pepper. I want to say that there was garlic involved, but that seems very unlikely, but why not? And garlic.

He mixed the bowl with a spoon. When the hot dogs were done boiling we fished them out with our fingers, part bravado, part not having tongs, and put them in buns. The fancy mixture was spooned on top. It was spicy and sweet and salty and fresh. Very tasty.

Growing up I loved hot dogs. Still do. When I was a teenager my mom would buy nacho cheese by the gallon and I had an obsession with spreading this cheese on white bread and putting a hot dog in the middle, at an angle to the corners, and microwaving it until it was just right. I don't think I ever did get it just right, but I came pretty close. The trick was to catch the hot dog right before the tips split and the hot dog bent and burst, which would make it rubbery and shriveled. It was a waiting game. Took a lot of focus. 28 seconds in that particular microwave. But you also wanted the cheese to be hot. And the bread would dry out if you didn't put the cheese all the way to the crust. Which means there were three different densities to consider.

Also at that time the Mini Mart had both chili and cheese, so if you could afford it you could get a sweet "dugout," a styrofoam container chili dog, that would last you all night as you rode your skateboard up and down Main Street.

But I digress. These are modern times, and as such, I must give you a modern recipe.

Hot Dogs For The Road

Just two days ago the Publisher and her daughter came to town. We spent the night before watching theater. They stayed the night in Harlem where I am living. My girlfriend lives there too. We are subletting until the 1st of April. The Publisher lives in Vermont. Her daughter is five, I think. My girlfriend came to meet us after the show. The Publisher's daughter loves my girlfriend. There was a party in the lobby after the show. The Publisher and her daughter went to Harlem not long after the show was finished. Me and my girlfriend stayed behind and ended up going to a bar. When we got home the Publisher came out of the room she and her daughter were staying in. We drank whiskey from a flask and red wine. There was nice conversation. Quick conversation. Soon we were all in bed, asleep.

In the morning, by 8 a.m., we were all up and going about business. My girlfriend went to work. I made tacos for the Publisher and a pancake for her daughter. Our associate from Norway came over. She drank coffee. Black. We talked business. This was nice.

I needed to go to work though [Apartment Renovation]. The Publisher needed to get back to Vermont [Publisher Work], and our Norwegian Associate had city business to take care of [Theatre Work]. The Publisher's daughter was still hungry though. There was talk of a second breakfast. The second breakfast was a hot dog wrapped in a pancake. A Pig In A Blanket.

Method

My Girlfriend likes pancakes. She keeps mixed batter in the fridge. I like pancakes too. I like that she does this.

First: Take pancake batter from the fridge. Put it on counter. Take the lid off. Heat up a skillet. Medium. Take butter from fridge. Add a hank to the skillet. Watch it melt for a while while talking about business.

Next: Realize the batter needs more water. Add water. Mix it with a fork. When it starts acting like crepe batter pour it into the skillet.

Next: Take the hot dogs out of the fridge. They will be cheese hot bogs you bought for your daughter that it turns out she doesn't like anymore. Take a moment to wonder if this is true, or if maybe she is going through a change in life that maybe she doesn't know how to tell you about. Remember she is ten years old thinking this will explain things. It won't.

Next: Flip the pancake. It will stick to the bottom of the pan. You didn't use enough butter.

Next: Take a plate from the cupboard. Put a hot dog on it. Microwave for seconds. You will hear a sizzling when it is done. Take it out of the microwave. It will be slightly bent. Try not to be ashamed of this. You miscalculated is all.

Next: Find the tinfoil in one of the drawers and unroll a 10-inch sheet. Eviscerate the sheet and lay it on the counter. Put the pancake on top. Put the hot dog on top of the pancake. Add a little maple syrup that your girlfriend got for Christmas and roll into burrito-like treat. Wrap the tinfoil around it. Tear the tinfoil down until the edge is exposed. Hand it over. The Publisher's daughter will scoff at you, don't worry, your Norwegian Associate will ask for a bite which will make the Publisher's daughter become jealous when she finds it is actually tasty.

Next: Do the same again because your Norwegian Associate will want one too.

Next: Send everybody on their way and take a shower.

Finally: Have a sense that everything is good and amazing when you have excellent people in your life.

Lesson

Sometimes things actually work out.

NOTES ON A COUPLE SPICES

Salt

Salt has a bad reputation. The body needs salt. The body needs salt to function. For the muscles to function. For nerves. For the blood to function. If you don't get enough you become ill. There is a reason you crave salt. A reason a deer will lick the ground where you piss. A reason huge blocks of it are placed in the areas cows graze. Too much is too much, of course. The reason you can't drink from the ocean is it takes more water to filter the salt in it through your kidneys than there is in the volume of water you are drinking in the first place. You just end up dehydrated. Which is way worse than not having enough salt. The ratio is off.

But in the hospital, the ratio is correct. Saline drips are nearly 1% salt. These are used to treat dehydration, see what I am getting at? I'm not advocating for Big Salt, I am just saying, you need it, stop worrying about it. Give salt a break. If you are eating too much salt you will be the first to know about it. You'll probably end up in the hospital, in excruciating pain, with a saline drip in your arm.

Black Pepper

Black pepper is overrated. It's tasty on salads and most dairy based things, like cheese and cream sauces, but for the most part it seems like a lame joke only the English would make:
Where does the Queen keep her armies?
Up her sleevies.
I feel like the whole reason we use black pepper on everything is because the English think it's spicy. They also boil celery. Not that black pepper can't be spicy, you just need to add it to water-based dishes, like soup, and if you add too much, it just tastes like black pepper, which is a good flavor, it's just a flavor that doesn't belong to anything you would be cooking. It's a tangent, to put it in math terms. A vector, to put it in physics terms. Aberrant, to put it in psychological terms. It's a flavor that only references its origins. A distraction.
Exceptions:

Chicken and black pepper
Lemon and black pepper
Steak and black pepper
Pepperoni pizza and black pepper

Oregano

I personally don't care for oregano. Use it like you want, but leave me out of it. I have heard of a Mexican oregano, which sounds tasty. Mexico is a desert. Desert oregano. Exotic. As it is though, the spice is just a way to make something "Italian." I am talking about dried oregano. I have been to Italy, and I don't remember eating anything that tasted of dried oregano. However, I do know of a way to cook the dried oregano taste out of jarred tomato sauce, so maybe it's about method.

Trickle-down economics didn't work in Italy either?

Oh, Reagan? No.

Cumin

Cumin is the B.O. of spices. Body odor. You could easily say that onions hold that title, but onions are more of a flavor than a spice. Cumin is good. I use it as little as possible, but it comes in handy when you can't find the way to make something taste right. Like chili. Like beans. Like pork chops. The problem with cumin is that, like black pepper, and in a bigger way, it alters the flavor of a dish to the point that it can only be one thing. Not that all dishes should be mercurial. Add cumin, you have a cumin dish. Add smoked paprika, you have a smoked paprika dish. Just be aware. All I am saying.

Garlic

Garlic is neutral. There is a thing as too much garlic, but that is only when it is raw. Raw garlic is aggressive. Like a general in an Army. All idea with none of the legwork. You could take it out with a sniper and the job would still get done, but it wouldn't be the same afterwards. But if you put too many generals on the battleground, things get confused. The Army suffers.

When adding garlic to things like salsa and salad dressing go easy, or eat a clove of garlic and see where it gets you. Grossed out, probably.

Cooked garlic is more subtle. It boils down. In water. In sauces. I think the reason they tell you to smash garlic with a knife is to reduce it's intensity, which I think only means that garlic particles are strongest when they are cluttered together, otherwise they are strangely wimpy, almost flaccid. When was the last time you ate a garlic soup?

Fried garlic is problematic. Bitter. You can ruin an entire dish by burning garlic. I think the saying is:

"Cook from both sides, but don't break the fire in half."

Recipe For Garlic Salt

They sell garlic in loaves. I never know what to make of this. Garlic is cheap, so I don't really question it, but who needs six bulbs of garlic at a time? I love having fresh garlic at hand, but what use is it when it starts growing stems? I mean, I understand there are uses for garlic stems, but that was never the point.

Here is a way to get around Big Garlic without too much effort:

Tools

Clove of garlic
Salt
Oil (vegetable)
Cutting board
Knife
Sheet of tin foil
Paper towels
Small plate
Cooking pan
Oven

Preparation

Set your oven to 210°F.

Place a garlic bulb on top of your cutting board.

Cut the top ¼ inch off of the sprouting garlic bulb you were forced to buy because of Big Garlic and Big Salt interests.

Separate the cloves and remove the skins.

Cut the cloves into slivers.

Take the sheet of tin foil and place it on the cooking pan.

Take 2 fingers and spread as little oil as possible on the sheet of tinfoil.

Put the slivered cloves of garlic on the tinfoil.

Spread until the garlic slivers are flat.

Sprinkle salt on top.

Place in oven.

Cook until the slivers are brown. [Brown is relative, but anything darker than "brown" is burnt, and I don't know how to describe that. So, not white, not green, but something right after green.]

Put the paper towel on the plate.

Put brown garlic slivers on the paper towel.

Leave over night.

In the morning, put garlic slivers in a bowl.

Pulverize with a shot glass.

Therefore

Garlic salt is essential for things like garlic toast and pepperoni pizza with black pepper.

THE TACO BURGER

THE TACO BURGER

Fate is a funny thing. It belongs to perspective. Which belongs to philosophy. Which belongs to circumstance. Which belongs to luck. Yesterday was a funny day. Mondays are swimming days. For my daughter, George. I pick her up from school at 3:30 p.m. and we take the B25 [Brooklyn twenty-five] bus down Fulton street to LIU [Long Island University]. Usually I am either working, or just waiting before I get on a train to get her. It takes an hour from Harlem by train. But yesterday I left early because I have this book coming out in March and we need a place to have a launch party. I was hoping to have it at the Performing Garage, but the Wooster Group is in tech all March. They told me suck a big fat fatty when I asked. Just joking. They were very nice, but they said no.

For the sake of not sounding like an asshole I will leave some details out. Not that I was being an asshole, or anybody else was being an asshole, it's just the words, "second option" seem so terribly crass. But the second option was down in the West Village. I left early to check it out. On the way to pick up my daughter and take her to swimming. The space was nice. It might work. I sent an email [electronic mail]. Still waiting to hear back.

But here's where fate kicks in. The site visit took literally one minute. I peeped through a window. Elderly people were doing stretches. I nodded. I walked away. I checked my phone to see what time it was as I descended the stairs into the courtyard. Two construction workers were talking to each other. I didn't catch what they were saying because I was distracted by how high and squeaky one of their voices was. They were both wearing orange safety vests.

It was still early. I had time to kill.

I decided to walk east. The weather was pleasant. Normally I would have just walked back the way I came. To the 14th Street stop on the C train, but because it was early I walked towards the West 4th Street stop. Down Bleecker street. I thought about this particularly moving passage in this book about Jack Kerouac called *Jack's Book*, where some journalist asks Jack:

"What is fame like?"

And his response:

"It's like yesterday's newspaper blowing down Bleecker Street."

I was hungry. I had enough time to get something to eat. I walked by this burger stand across the street from Greg Mehrten's apartment [he's from The Wooster Group]. I thought about stopping, but they always take too long. And, expensive. I kept walking.

Now I wanted a burger. A cheeseburger. McDonald's by NYU [New York University]. Dollar burgers, plus maybe chicken nuggets with honey mustard. I started actively looking for free newspapers to read. All the boxes I found were empty and filled with trash. There was a news kiosk across the street from the McDonald's. I bought a *Daily News*. My second option, *The Post*, had a cover that made me upset. I crossed the street and went inside.

The line was long. Standing in line is hard. The same thought. Over and over. Two cheeseburgers and a four-piece chicken nugget with honey mustard. Two cheeseburgers and a four-piece chicken nugget with honey mustard.

Then

"Next in line."

"Hi, can I get two cheeseburgers and a four-piece chicken nugget with–"

"You want any sauce?"

"Uh, yeah, um, honey mustard." I had a whole speech prepared. Denied.

"$3.26."

I gave her four dollars. She gave me 74 cents in change. Her receipt machine was broken so she had to use the cashier's next to her. #355.

The next guy ordered a coffee. I stood by the trashcans. The next guy ordered a coffee too. There was an upstairs. The first guy that ordered the coffee was baffled that they didn't have sweet tea. He couldn't believe what kind of operation they were running here. I nodded. I can't remember the last time I was in a McDonald's that was empty. Or efficient. I felt complicit and was trying to ignore the fact that what I was doing was tacit. American. It was easy, actually. When they called my number I took my bag and sat by the window. It was nice. I read the newspaper. The cheeseburgers made me sweat. I was done by 2:48 p.m.

But here is where fate really kicks in. I finished the two cheeseburgers and four-piece chicken nuggets with honey mustard. Then the trash. Next, the door. I crossed the street and went down into the subway.

Two years ago I was rushing to get to the recording studio so I could record some vocals before I got on a plane to Norway. I was carrying a huge duffel bag. My glasses at the time fell apart constantly. The lens would fall out. The right one. To this day I carry a small screwdriver in my wallet because of it. When I got on the train I pulled the bag over my head. My glasses fell on the floor. A man who looked like this bass player named David picked up my glasses for me. The lens had fallen out. By the time I put the lens back in and could get a good look, he had left the train. This was a good omen. The recording went wonderful.

But then yesterday, as I was standing on the train platform. There he was. [Also, on good authority it wasn't him the first time.]

Not that I talked to him, or that it even matters that I talked to him, but the point is that it happened. Had I not left early to check out the space. Had I not decided to walk down Bleecker street. Had I not walked by Greg Mehrten's [from The Wooster Group] and got hungry for cheeseburgers. Had I not known about that McDonald's. Had I not been lured in. Had there not have been a line. Newspaper. Sweet tea. #3920.

I guess my point is

When I made tacos for a living it was for a restaurant/chain called Taco John's. The best item on the menu was a Taco Burger. It was a taco within a hamburger bun. It was sweet and salty and spicy. Almost nobody ever bought one. I think a bag of eight hamburger buns lasted two weeks. And I ate half. The last time I was in Wyoming they decided to discontinue them. With great fanfare. "Last chance!" they said. On the billboard. They brought the Taco Burger back after a month due to public outcry. Hate to see you be a bridesmaid, love to watch you put two in the bush.

Taco Burger

Ingredients

1 pound of ground beef
1 package of taco seasoning [Ortega is the best because the package looks the coolest. Old El Paso kind of tastes better.]
1 head of iceberg lettuce
1 package of sharp cheddar cheese
1 package of hamburger buns [8-pack]
Salt
Pepper
Hot sauce
Water

Tools

Spoon
Knife
Scissor
Cutting board
Cheese grater
Plate

Method

In a medium skillet, brown ground beef. Stir with spoon. Add salt and pepper to taste.

When beef is browned and seasoned cut top

from taco seasoning and dump on top. Fill the empty package with water. Pour into skillet. Stir with spoon.

Cook until the water evaporates. Stirring often.

When the water is evaporated turn off heat.

Let sit.

While meat sits remove plastic packaging from lettuce. Also remove the top two layers of leaves and throw into the trash. Whack the stem against the cutting board, remove. Throw the stem into the trash.

Using the knife, cut a chunk from the head. Slice chunk into small slivers. Set aside.

Using the knife, cut open the cheese. Peel the plastic packaging back to about the middle.

Using the grater, grate a good deal of cheese. This is a taste thing, do what you think is the right amount. I find that more is better, you can always put the remnants in a container and put into the fridge for later.

Open the package of buns. Remove one bun. Place on the plate. If the bun package has a wire tie or a plastic c-square I feel it is best to throw this away. Just twist the top of the bag and it under itself. Nobody needs a middleman.

Open the bun.

Spoon meat onto the bottom half of the bun.

Sprinkle cheese on top.

Add hot sauce to taste.

Add lettuce slivers. A little more than a pinch, but less than a pile.

Cover with the top half of the bun.

Press down.
Enjoy.

Jingle

"There's whole lot of Mexican going on, going on at Taco John's."

FILING FOR CHAPTER 11

I'm not poor, I took a vow of poverty. Or maybe it should be; I'm not broke, I took a vow of poverty. The implications are different. Being broke means you don't have any money at the moment. Being poor means you will never have any money. You're a blight on society. I'm not broke, I'm poor.

Soon after my daughter was born I was homeless. I was living in a garage in Williamsburg that had been converted into a performance space. I guess that sounds like a home, but it wasn't a home. Maybe a domicile. I slept on the plywood floor. I had a camping pad my brother Luke had lent me. I had a sleeping bag that my brother lent me as well. I used my coat as a pillow. It was November. There was a heater, but it was expensive to use. Out of respect I only used it when necessary. I wasn't paying the bills.

I ate peanut butter on corn tortillas. I cooked the tortillas on a work light that had a cage. The work light could get hot enough to start a fire. The cage was a precaution.

I bathed in a bucket. I could wash my balls and

my butt and my feet and my face and my armpits. There was a sink and a toilet. I used dishwashing liquid. There was also an unlimited supply of shit beer in aluminum bottles that had been donated to one of the theater groups that worked there for one of their shows. A pregnant woman would chop the bottles in half with an axe onstage. The beer was gross and made me feel like shit, but nobody sleeps in a garage converted to a performance space sober, right?

One day I started bleeding from my ears. I was 31 and the only pain I was in was psychological. I asked Jay, Jay who was older than me; Jay, who played drums in this band, Dishwashers, that I sang for; Jay, who drank more than anyone I knew:

"You ever bleed from your ears?"

"Yeah, only when I am dehydrated."

We were sitting at a bar that I hated. He was buying me drinks that weren't gross and warm. That didn't come from an aluminum can stacked under a riser in a garage that had been converted into a performance space.

I was gross and smelly. I was broke. I hadn't washed my clothes in over two weeks. I had told him a story about getting on a train earlier that day:

"But come on, I had used my shit, I mean, the rest of my change, the change to get on the train, nickels even, and it was the J-Z, so it was above ground, and I sat down, and I stunk so much the teenagers next to me got up and moved away."

"Nah, you don't stink so much, why didn't you just ride your bike? Hey babe, a couple more if you don't mind, shot?" He was talking to the bartender, then to me.

"Yeah, sure."

"Hit the head." Jay got up. He hit the head. On his way back he played some music on the jukebox. I watched him. I smelled myself. I did stink so much. The bartender left us two beers and two shots of whiskey on the bar. Took money from the stack Jay had left. I wanted to grab that money and run out the door. I didn't. Jay came back and sat down. He looked as drunk as I felt. He said:

"Cheers, fuck-face." He was holding the shot.

"Cheers." I took the shot and nearly puked. His song came on. He laughed, "Lightweight. You still sleeping on the floor of the Hole?"

"Yeah. You ever bleed from your ears?"

"Yeah, only when I am dehydrated. Ma'am, another shot, Joe?"

"I can't"

"Pussy."

I was a pussy. I was drunk, too. The only thing I had eaten in three days was peanut butter and corn tortillas. I smelled like a bum. I had my bike. I had a rule with my bike:

Don't ride your bike when you are drunk.

The problem with that logic is that the second you are drunk you abandon that logic. We sat there for a while. In silence. Jay got up to play more songs on the jukebox. I stood up and stumbled out onto the street. I unlocked my bike and got on. I didn't know where I was going. I had a couple choices. I could go south and get yelled at for being drunk, get kicked to the curb. End up back where I started. I could go back to the garage and find that balance without even trying in the first place. Or I could go north and meet another asshole that I knew. Maybe a new perspective.

I was riding my bike south on Broadway when I changed my mind. I turned around. An asshole with a new perspective was better than being stuck between a drunk and an asshole kicking me to the curb. I got one block before everything changed.

I remember seeing a gap between two parked cars. The next thing I knew I was on a spineboard. Then nothing. They were loading me into an ambulance. Then nothing. Then I was on a stretcher. They were pushing me down the hallway of the hospital. Then nothing. I woke up on a clean bed. Under clean sheets. There was a tray of food on top of a cart that could swivel over my chest. Perpendicular to the bed. The phone was ringing.

Why there was a phone next to my bed is still confusing. Luxury confounds. I guess it is because I am white. I could sue. I was broke, not poor.

The phone call didn't help. The mother of my child said:

"Shit, you're alive."

"Yeah, I suppose."

"Can you take George on Friday? I got a thing."

"Yeah, ok."

"Great!"

My shoulder was broken. My friend Ramona let me sleep on her couch until I got better. She even did my laundry. Very nice. But between then and this, let me explain what it is like being homeless and poor as apposed to being a renter and broke:

Method

Hunger changes things. Being hungry makes you desperate. Desperation changes your behavior.

When

You are hanging out with your daughter and she is just one year old and she needs to take a nap, and when she is sleeping, you eat a couple cracker slabs of her mom's foie gras and her mom comes home and tells you to stop eating that shit because it is expensive. And you're homeless. And the last thing you ate was a corn tortilla with peanut butter cooked on a work light.

As

You are homeless.

Or

I'm not poor, I'm an artist.

I'm

Just saying.

A RECIPE FOR DISASTER

Cara Tobin. Just saying her name adds a little spice to the air. I guess you could call her my first love, although I don't think love really factored into things. One day I didn't know who she was, the next she was my girlfriend and I couldn't get rid of her. I honestly don't remember meeting her. She was 17. I was 20. Bonfire, probably. Maybe a house party. She was an orphan. Half-Irish, half-Native American. Bipolar. She had red hair and was really good at doing handstands. From Worland, my hometown.

I liked her pretty good. She was always entertaining. A huge pain in the ass to everyone I knew, which I really liked. You literally could not take her anywhere without thinking about it first.

She was still in high school. Wore too much makeup. Huge tits. No ass. Was a cheerleader because all the popular girls quit cheerleading for some reason, I can't remember the reason, but I am sure it was dumb, like one of the Crawford girls got a B in horticulture and couldn't ride on the homecoming float.

But this was great. The squad was ragtag.

Greasy and hairy and angry and ugly. Cara was the prettiest. I don't think I would ever use the word pretty to describe her. She wasn't the captain though. That was Birdie. Birdie was the best. A square. As tall as she was wide. Wonderful to talk to. The cutest little mustache. I am pretty sure she was a genius.

They were banned from the football games and the basketball games. The idea was because of the protest, but I think it was just because people are cruel and these beauties were a rough lot.

They could cheer at the wrestling matches though. Which was hilarious because my dad loved watching wrestling. I would go to these matches just to watch him watch the girls get worked up on the side of mats. Pounding and clapping and actually caring. Greasy hair and bad skin. Misshapen. Under weight and over weight at the same time. Sweating. My dad had a very specific idea about how things should look. This was not that. He would get so distracted that he had to leave early on many occasions. I saw it twice. He told me about it afterward not knowing that I watched him. I think his words were:

"I can't believe they let them get away with that shit. It just makes my blood boil." Then he would go outside and spend the next hour folding a brown canvas tarp that was the size of our lawn by himself. Shaking his head, and sighing.

I wasn't doing so good myself. Cara was hilarious, but she was changing my life. I needed some time to think. She wasn't helping me think. She was doing the opposite.

I decided to break up with her. I took her to coffee. Halfway through breaking up with her I had my first panic attack. I went blind. My skin hurt. I ran out into the parking lot. I must have gotten into her car because the next thing I knew I was under a tree with my head on her lap. She was stroking my hair.

I decided to stay with her. We decided to go to college together. She was about to graduate. I got my GED and took my entrance exams. My brother Luke was already at the University. We got an apartment with him and his girlfriend in the tech part of town above a Mormon family with six kids. A house. We had our own door. A living room. Two bedrooms. A kitchen and a bathroom. Two cats. A television. A banana chair and cable.

I started school in the fall. Cara decided not to go to school. She moved in with a friend of ours near the campus. She refused to get a job. She had some money saved up from working at the A&W in Worland. When that money ran out she got kicked out of her apartment and moved in with me. I didn't like this. My brother Luke didn't like this. His girlfriend didn't like this. I still wanted to break up with her. She had no money. She refused to get a job. She ate all the food. Didn't do her dishes, and was kind of bonkers, like all the time.

I tried to ditch her constantly. I tried to convince her she was a lesbian. No luck. That she wanted a dude with a bigger thing than mine. Mine was perfect. That we didn't get along. But I can change! But it's not working, we need to stop. I don't want to stop! I love you! I love you too, but no more!

Aside from knowing it was wrong being together, she really did refuse to get a job. In order to pay the rent I was working full-time and going to school full-time. I would get up at 7 a.m. and get home at 11 p.m. She would be asleep when I woke up, eat all the food all day, dishes included, and then be smoking a bowl at night when I got home, rocking in the banana chair, watching re-runs of *Murphy Brown*. I know it sounds cute now, but it made me so angry.

When I finally insisted that she had to move out and I didn't care where she was going, she got in her car and drove next to me all the way to campus at three miles an hour, crying and begging to let her stay.

I must be an asshole, because to this day I feel bad about forcing her out of my life. Her problems are so much darker than mine. She became a prostitute in Seattle. Got addicted to crack. Has a child she ditched on her parents' door. I don't think that is the order of the way it happened, but it is what happened. I wish her the best.

However

Cara had a preternatural ability to know where

I was at all times. It was very impressive. I had it too, but only because I could feel her knowing where I was. Shortly after breaking up with her I went to this bar called The Buckhorn. The dead of winter in Wyoming. Everything was covered in frost. Cars didn't start. If they did start, you spent 10 minutes scraping the ice off your windshield. Then you spent another 10 minutes with your heater blaring with your hands underneath your legs waiting for your car to heat up. There was no other way around it. And Laramie is at 10,000 feet. At the mouth of the Rockies.

Next

I walked into the bar. It was a Friday night and The Buckhorn was packed. I met my brother and suddenly something felt off. I knew I had to leave. The back door was the way to get in if you were underage. I dipped out. It was a long cold walk, but I was trying to avoid drama. When I got home I didn't turn any lights on. I brushed my teeth and sat down on my bed. The next thing I know there was footsteps on the roof. Followed by a banging on the window. I panicked and ran out the front door just as my brother Luke was coming in. I said I was sorry and ran as fast as I could to my friend Mike's house.

Turns Out

Cara got into the bar from the back door. When she saw my brother Luke she knew I had ditched. She ran out to her car and started it. She couldn't see through the windshield because of the ice. She rolled her window down and drove with her head sticking out. At some point she hit a culvert, or a deep drainage dip, and broke the front axle of her car. The car stopped working so she jumped out and started running down the road. When she got to our house she must have done some sort of gymnastics and hopped onto the roof. She ran across the roof and started banging on the window. Just then I was running out the front door as my brother was coming up the stairs.

He calmed her down. I slept at a friend's.

Last

The last two times I saw her were funny. The first time she said she liked to fuck black dudes with big dicks. The second, she was pregnant and doing a handstand around a bonfire.

She Was

Bad News.

BACON

"The key to life is looking at it in the past tense. It was what it was. I like the cut of your jib, man." – Lurky ["Uranus Is Nice"]

The last time I ever talked to my father was on my mom's cell phone in a hotel room in Oklahoma. He called specifically to talk to me. He pretended the reason he called was to just check up on us, but that wasn't how he did business. He was calling to say goodbye. He was dying. He wouldn't admit it, but he was dying. I think he must have known that I would understand because the conversation was jobic in the sense that we were finding common ground through suffering. The conversation was both inane and profound. I had never, not once, talked to my father on the telephone. It was like watching him ride a bicycle. Outside of the scope.

It was around nine in the morning. My mom was curling her hair. I was sitting on the edge of the bed staring at the television. Drinking coffee. Her father, my grandfather, was the master of ceremonies at a bluegrass festival in Guthrie, Oklahoma. That is why we were there. The phone rang. He must have called from a landline. I picture him standing on the carpet in his linesman's boots. Ready to get out the door. But me and my mom were on his mind. I am sure he said something like:

"Hey Peg, how did the drive go?"

"Ok. Little traffic outside Denver, but nothing to write home about. You finish the Heyser skull?"

"Yeah, had an extra Ivory. Put Joe on the horn." She turned to me holding out the phone, "Talk to your dad." I stood up and took the phone. She went back to curling her hair.

"Hey, Pops."

"You get in all right?"

"Pretty easy."

"How's New York? Doin' alright? Getting enough work?"

"Yeah, I guess. Kind of hard to find a balance between doing good work and money work, ya know?"

"Yeah, that's the rub. Eating enough?"

"I think so."

"Ok. Put your mom back on."

"Ok, bye, dad."

"Yes." I handed the phone back to my mom. I sat back down on the bed. I stared at the television. Drinking my coffee.

My dad was really bad at making bacon. It was always half burnt and half raw. My brother Luke is pretty good at it, but it takes him forever. I assume that it's a personality thing because it takes him forever to cook anything. I really can't figure out his brain. He has these big brown eyes that take in everything. Must be nice to be in that brain of his. But, god, he cooks so slowly.

Buck though, my oldest brother, he cooks a mean bacon. He cooks everything well. I think it is mostly attitude. Maybe it's because he is the first boy. Casual and cocky, he can get whatever the hell he wants. And maybe that explains Luke too. The last boy. Waiting and waiting and waiting. But Buck's method is simple:

Put the bacon on the grill. Turn the heat to low. Leave it the fuck alone until it is finished.

I very much agree with this method. But as a single father I really need to get the bacon cooked and dressed and out the door in 30 minutes, or less.

My daughter used to love bacon. I would ask her if she wanted it crispy and she would always say:

"I want it extra crispy!"

My girlfriend likes it that way too. Two peas in a posture. Who am I to deny them? But it takes a little work. This is the method that keeps everybody happy.

Buying The Bacon

Bacon comes in pounds. Cheaper bacon is best. Artisanal bacon is a joke. Expensive ham. Good bacon doesn't rot. It molds. It should be salty and full of sulfites. You should be able to eat it like jerky, raw. Wet, slimy jerky. Like a week old jib. Flapping in the breeze.

Opening The Bacon

Use a scissor. Bacon is cured. It is always old. They package it hermetically to keep the bugs out. It can store for weeks in the refrigerator. Treat it like cheese. Don't eat the mold.

Cooking

Bacon starts long, but finishes short. A little like sleeping with an old man. It wants to keep going, but ends up getting distracted and falling asleep.

Bacon is half fat and half meat. It cooks at two different temperatures. It is also cured. This is good. This means it won't cook when it is boiled. It will heat up, of course, but the structure of the meat won't change.

Method

Lay as many strips of bacon as you can in the biggest frying pan you have. Cover the bacon in water. Turn the heat to high. Bring to a boil. The temperature of the meat and the fat will equalize as the water evaporates. When the sound of the cooking switches from a boiling noise to a frying noise turn the heat to low. Flip the bacon immediately. If you don't it will stick to the bottom of the pan.

The rest of the cooking is a waiting game. The fat will render and fry the bacon. You can either leave it alone, as Buck would do, and end up with a pan full of variety bacon. Crispy, burnt, and raw. Or drop the heat to nearly nothing and spend the next hour making perfect bacon, as Luke would do. Or you could just play with it, and end up somewhere in between like I do.

The Most Important Thing

The most important thing about bacon is draining it. If you don't put it on paper towels when it is finished it ends up greasy and gross. If you can afford bacon you can afford paper towels. If you can't afford bacon you will probably want as much of that grease as there is.

Irrespective

Pour the leavings in a glass jar. Put it in the refrigerator. A salty and flavorful oil. Perfect for eggs and beans.

VERTICAL MEATS

GRAVITY JUICE FROM A VERTICAL MEAT [SEVEN DOLLAR BANK TACO]

Spirit. Spirit of thought, mostly, is essential. I want to make a reference to something I read, but I don't want to mention the thing itself, so I won't. I will say the ending sums it up pretty good:

"Every now and then you run up on one of those days when everything's is in vain ... a stone bummer from start to finish; and if you know what's good for you, on days like these you sort of hunker down in a safe corner and watch. Maybe think a bit. Lay back on a cheap wooden chair, screened off from the traffic, and shrewdly rip the poptops out of five or eight Budweisers."

A day like today, a night like last night.

I woke up early because I went to bed early. I had every intention of sleeping as much as possible. I woke up so hungry I almost threw up. I got up and pissed. I splashed some water on top of the 20 black beans caked to the bottom of the pot that was on top of the stove. I lit the burner. Set it to high. I took the iceberg lettuce from the fridge and chopped a hunk off. Took a slice of American cheese and unwrapped it. I took the corn tortillas out of the fridge. I took two from the package. I turned on the back burner. To high. I threw the tortillas on the flame. Took a spoon and aggravated the bottom of the bean pot. I flipped the tortillas. Chopped the lettuce. Flipped the tortillas. Stirred the beans.

When the tortillas were steaming, I put the slice of cheese between them. I turned off the heat to the beans. I flipped the tortillas one more time. I turned off the flame.

The small plate I took from the cupboard was just slightly bigger than the tortillas. The cheese seemed melted. The two tortillas with cheese in between fit nicely. I spooned all 20 black beans on top. There was a little sauce as well. I scraped that over the beans. I sprinkled some salt on top. Added some green hot sauce and the chopped iceberg lettuce.

I ran the faucet for a second and filled a pint glass with cold water. I went back to bed. I ate the taco lying down. My computer was open. I was naked.

I remember taking a drink of water. Then I remember closing my eyes. Then I remember hearing:
"Peg."
"Yes?"
"This is important."
"Ok, yes?"

"I just refilled the ice trays, try not to jostle the refrigerator."
Then I was asleep.

***

Last night had been fun. It ended around midnight. My timing was good. It took less than an hour to get home. I stopped at a deli between the train and the apartment. I bought coffee and hot chips.

Earlier there had been pizza. Mushroom and truffle oil. Truffle oil just tastes like bad breath to me. But it did make me hungry. When I got home I cooked up a sausage patty. I ate it on top of two cooked tortillas. Cooked meaning heated up over flames on top of the stove. Also, some black beans. Which led to only 20 being left behind. Also, some chopped up iceberg lettuce. Also, I chopped the sausage patty into chunks. Also, there was a slice of cheese. Also, this is why I was so hungry in the morning, don't go to sleep with a full stomach. Also, I was lying on the bed naked. Also, I fell asleep without brushing my teeth. Also, this was why I spit blood in the morning when I brushed my teeth.

The hot chips were tasty. The taco was tasty. I slept soundly. I woke up hungry. I almost puked. I made myself a taco and went back to sleep.

***

I woke up the second time. I made some coffee. I read the papers. I took a shower. Fed the fish. Watered the plants. I needed to go to the bank and deposit some money.

[I also had $7.58 in my bank account that I needed to use. My bank charges me $8.95 if my balance is less than $300, so if I don't use that money it makes a very rich man a tiny bit richer. Not only that, but the point of banks is that the agreement is: You lend them your money so they can invest it. And the idea that they charge you to use your money to make themselves more money is so absurd I could punch somebody. But because this is so insane, and this is where government is actually useful, they can't take more money than you have in your account to pay their own fees for using your money to make themselves more money.]

The streets were filled with children. It took some work to wade through them. School just let out. My timing stank. It took 10 minutes to navigate the block. Young kids though. Not angry yet. Not a single cigarette or a mustache among them.

I took a right at the end of the block. Walked up to the bank. The bank was empty. The transaction was complex, but nice. I left with a receipt. I took a right and went into the grocery store. I had $7.58 to spend.

I knew I had tortillas at home. Corn. I also knew that pork was cheap at this market. My plan was to get $4.00 of pork chops. $2.00 of cheese. And use the rest for jalapenos and onions. I ended up paying $7.25 for 3 pork chops, 8 ounces of sharp cheddar cheese, 2 jalapenos, and 1 red salad onion.

***

A few days ago I had some plans to write. This usually involves drinking beer and pacing around. But lately I have been too sensitive. But because of this plan, I had a bunch of beer in the refrigerator to drink. When I got home, I put the groceries on the counter. Before long I was pacing around. I put the cheese in the refrigerator. I knew I would shred it. Cold cheese shreds, warm cheese crumbles. I let the pork chops warm up. I opened a beer and stopped thinking.

Seven Dollar Bank Taco

Tacos are always good. They are really easy. A Mexican sandwich. Although a Mexican sandwich is a torta, and a torta is an American sandwich. Criss-cross applesauce. White bread is bunk. Judging by digestion. A butt anchor.

Ingredients

3 dollars of pork
2.50 [two-and-a-half] dollars of cheese [sharp]
1 dollar of jalapenos
1 dollar of red salad onions
Salt

White vinegar
Sugar
Garlic salt [see Chapter 9, "Notes On A Couple Spices"]
Water
Slab of butter
Spoon of bacon grease
Leftover corn tortillas
Leftover iceberg lettuce
Cast-iron skillet
Bowl
Smaller owl
Bunch of beer

Method

Open a beer and forget about things. Pace around until you remember you left some pork on the counter. Put it in a bowl. Pour some white vinegar on top. Sprinkle with salt.

Let soak for an hour or so. When you get bored with your thoughts, go back into the kitchen and turn a burner to high and put the cast-iron skillet on top.

Add bacon grease and butter.

Chop onion. Chop jalepeno. Grate cheese. Cut up remaining Iceberg lettuce.

Fry pork. Modern pork is hard to understand. Fry one side until brown. Turn over. Fry other side until nearly brown. Depending on the color of the pork in the beginning, it will either be soft or hard to the touch. Cook it until it makes you nervous that it might be overcooked.

Fork into the smaller bowl. Vertically.

At this point the frying pan should be smoking. Add some water to the bowl with the vinegar and salt, the one you used for the pork. Add the homemade garlic powder and some sugar. Stir with a fork. Deglaze the frying pan. Cook until the liquid is half reduced. Turn off the flame.

As the meat sits, wonder if the fact that it is sitting vertically will affect where the juices collect. It must, right? Gravity.

Dish

Get distracted by writing the recipe and forget to actually eat the food.

However

Does it matter how you place the meat you cook when it is done? It must. Does that mean we should rotisserize?

Because

Set it, and forget it.

THE TEN DOLLAR WEEK

One good thing about getting older is your metabolism slows down. I can go two days without eating before I notice I'm starving. I think part of it is the fact that you gather so much shit in your system that your body is too busy trying to flush it out that it doesn't notice that nothing new is coming in. That, and contrary to popular belief, you won't die if you miss a meal or two. Especially breakfast.

I used to get high from not eating [I'm sure I have mentioned this before], not anymore though. I just get hangnails and can't sleep properly. I dream of food, mostly steaks, but lately I have been dreaming of tomatoes. Explain that. I hate tomatoes. I think I'm allergic.

Money issues are usually resolved by working. Work, however, is a nebulous term. Nobody is going to pay me for working on my next novel, or working on a hangover. I can work up an appetite, but the only way to pay for that is with food. I guess I am talking about a job, but even that term is nebulous. I was looking for work, but I found a job. It was a hand-job.

I got work this week. A job. All day, every day. Monday to Friday. My daughter and her mom went on tour. But I am severely broke at the moment. I had a moment of panic. Usually if I am starving I see my daughter every day after school, so if necessary I can finish her lunch. And two days of the week I stay with her so her mom can go out and I can eat dinner at their house. But with them gone I am suddenly out of resources. I had the option to take care of the cat and the hamster, Shiver and Peony, but their apartment makes me uneasy, and I have been staying in this sweet pad in Harlem that has a room I can write in. Also my girlfriend is out of town, so I have nothing but time to myself. To write. Also, somebody else said they could do it.

I messed up though. They have cupboards and cupboards of food that I could eat. Crackers, tuna, cookies, ramen. Things in the freezer. Cheeses and olives. Breads that will go bad. It would be my duty to raid the larders. It is immoral to let food go to waste. But what's done is done.

So here I am with $10 to my name and a week of work to get through. The Publisher was here on Tuesday. She worries about my eating. She left me some sausage from her farm, 12 eggs. A hunk of cheese. A stack of bacon. And two bags of coffee. Three cans of beans, two black, one pink. And a 12-pack of light beer.

I ate all the cheese, the bacon, and almost all of the eggs. The sausage too, delicious. The coffee is holding strong. The beer was gross, but gone. The black beans, gone. The pink beans I have yet to explore.

Earlier today I went to Williamsburg to get a couple of birds. Parakeets. They need a home for a week while the owner is out of town. Cute birds. As I was travelling with them on the subway I played my money situation over in my head. I could get two cans of black beans, one hunk of cheese, and one package of burrito-sized tortillas that come in packages of eight. This means I could make two burritos a day through Thursday, or make two burritos on Monday, one on Tuesday, two on Wednesday, one on Thursday, and two on Friday. Or maybe two on Thursday, and one on Friday, it being the end of the week and all.

Before I left to get the birds I had stacked all the quarters I had into piles of four. There were 17 piles. I normally don't hold on to change. Not because I am a miser, but because I am poor. I'm not poor, I took a vow of poverty. I dropped the birds off and went directly to the supermarket. I took five dollars in quarters with me. Just in case. Also, I knew I would probably write later, and writing without beer, for me, is like fucking without a hard-on, you can get the job done on one side, but not the other.

I bought the tortillas, and the cheese, and the beans. $8.66. I stopped at the deli and got two Coors tall boys. $4. I was annoyed with the cost. It should have been $3.50, but the guy was nice and things are what they are. We talked about the weather. It was a sunny day. The snow was melting.

Here is where the story comes back together:

I hadn't eaten all day. I was very hungry, but I also wanted to start cooking the meals for the rest of the week. There were four strips of bacon remaining. I cut them into 1/2-inch chunks. I put them in the frying pan and added water. I would use this bacon later, but I didn't know what for. I cut the Publisher's sausage into 1/2-inch chunks as well. I wanted the meat to be hot, but I wasn't trying to cook it. I grated some cheese that I had bought since the Publisher's cheese ran out. I made two tacos with the remaining taco-sized tortillas I still had. I added lettuce I had as well, iceberg. Black pepper and hot sauce. The tacos were tasty.

You shouldn't cook when you are hungry. You shouldn't shop when you are hungry. It taints your vision. I wasn't hungry when I finished cooking the bacon. I wanted the grease, mostly. Also, I had moved on to the idea of writing this. I rendered the bacon grease and removed the chunks of flesh. I would use those later, for what, I don't know. I opened both cans of beans and poured them into the pan. I fill both cans half full with water and stirred with a spoon. I dumped the water in the pan. But, rice.

I don't like rice. Vapor food, like celery. But I will give it another chance. There was rice in the cupboard, thanks Jonny! I started a cup of rice with three cups of water. Brought it to a boil. Covered it. Started to pace.

The rice was cooking. The beans were cooking. The birds were chirping. I was pacing. I sat down to write this and the sound of things being ready came to my ears. The smells, as well. I stirred the beans and turned the heat off. I took the lid off the rice and put it back on. I turned the heat off. I sat down and started typing. The words I wrote were:

"One good thing about getting older is that your metabolism slows down..."

So:

The Ten Dollar Week

Idea

Run out of money and have to live for a week while working a laborious job.

Thought

A burrito a day is enough food as long as it has the basic elements of nutrition:

Protein
Dairy
Fiber
Salts

Ingredients

2 cans of black beans
1 hunk of cheese
1 package of large tortillas
1 cup of rice

Method

First:

Cut all the bacon you have left in your refrigerator into chunks. Fry in a pan. Use your best self-discipline to not eat the cooked chunks of cooked bacon.

Then:

When this is done, remove the chunks of bacon from the pan and put in a bowl for later use.

Then:

Open the cans of beans and add to the oil that is left from the bacon. It will seem like a lot, but I swear to you the flavor itself will be worth it.

Then:

Start rice on the back burner. Use a 1 to 3 mixture. You will want a wet rice in the end.

Finally:

Pace around while the beans and rice cook. Stir often. If things seem undercooked add water, if they seem done, turn off the heat.

Tomorrow:

You will be faced with a dilemma, either make the burritos tonight or do it in the morning. I suggest spending the next hour making the rice taste better. Maybe add that last little butter you have and some spices. Plus, you have that spiced oil you made. But if you make the burritos tonight, they won't be as fresh tomorrow as they would be, but then you will save yourself 15 minutes in the morning, so you could get some more sleep.

So

The choice is yours. Extra sleep versus tastier food.

My Choice

See what the birds are up to, let them decide.

FEELINGS

My stupid mom is a jerk. It's not her fault though. She doesn't understand poverty the way I do. I am a jerk, too. I only understand poverty because I choose it. I have a privilege. A choice. A choice I made. I choose my life.

My mom is from Oklahoma. Middle class. My father was from Montana. Middle class. They met at college and got married and moved to Wyoming.

They both worked extremely hard. Humiliating jobs that they hated. There were moments of prosperity. Moments of terror that they tried to hide from me and my brothers. But we never starved. We always had a home. I don't remember not having food. Gross food, yes. Rabbit stew. Yuck. Stringy. All week? Mom!

I dropped out of school on my 17th birthday. I hitchhiked south, to Laramie. This was literally the day that the life I knew ended, and the life I now know, began. October 31, 1994.

I want to talk about starving and the disparity of thought.

Disclaimer

I hold nobody else aside from myself responsible for my own actions. Life is tricky. Agatha Christie: *"We were not put on this Earth to be safe."*

She believed in God. And I am paraphrasing. But, my point is:

Being poor is not easy. Nobody is suddenly poor. Going bankrupt just means you lose all your assets. Your standing in society. This seems cute to me. Because it is meaningless. *The Times* recently did a poll asking people if they would rather:

A: Be accused of doing something unconscionable that they didn't do.

Or,

B: Do something unconscionable that nobody ever found out about.

Seventy percent chose option B. Which, to me, means most people would rather murder somebody than be accused of a murder they didn't commit. Which seems crazy. It also says something about the power of society.

Being poor is a stigma. Being destitute somehow means a moral decline. Being desperate, however, removes you from the human race. There is no way to describe what it feels like to steal food. A combination of guilt and need. Like a junky. And then to somehow ask for help? I was on food stamps for a while until they kicked me off because I couldn't prove I was poor. Because

I had no paperwork. Because I had no work. Therefore, there was no reference. I understand that to a certain degree. But who the hell would spend the hours and hours it takes to get food stamps, standing in line, then waiting in the horribly depressing waiting room for the meeting with the person that will decide, and then meeting with this person whose entire modus is to deny you this little crumb of light that you might be able to eat in the near future. The only thing you can buy with food stamps is food. [Used to be you could buy a nickel candy and get change back because food stamps were actually currency and with that change you could buy whatever you wanted, smokes, booze, not no more.]

I want to go somewhere with this, but I am having trouble. It is really complex. I saw a guy the other day pick up a penny from the sidewalk. I also saw a guy drop a dime and just shrug and keep walking. I also saw a guy in the subway, just today, count out $53 that he had begged from people on the train. He kept saying, "You already pissed me off, I'm about to get angry." Being poor is stressful. It is a full-time job.

My choice to be poor only comes from my desire to be an artist. I fell asleep at some point when I was hopeful and ambitious, and woke up here. I have agency, though. Tomorrow could be different. Actually.

Point

Please just give a dollar to anyone who asks for it. If you have it. They need it more than you do. I do this myself, even with the knowledge that they most likely have more money than I do. Which is entertaining and frustrating. Being a pariah is not a choice. Remember that.

Rabbit Stew

There was a weird moment when my family was super poor and all the boys were old enough to hunt that we ate rabbit stew. Rabbits were easy to kill. Stupid and everywhere. I remember one time my brothers and dad coming back with a toboggan stacked with dead rabbits. The memory doesn't make sense because they must have dragged the toboggan from the alley, through the corridor that the fence and the garage created, and parked it by the back door. I'm not asking questions now, though. But why not carry the corpses? Must have been pride. If I remember right, they gutted them and skinned them on the gravel. But the guts though? They didn't make it into the stew.

First:

Hang out with your mom until your brothers and your dad bring back a toboggan sled of dead rabbits.

Then:

Watch them disembowel the carcasses. Peel the

skins off. Bring the naked bodies inside and stack them on the counter.

Then:

Watch your dad carve the meat off the bones while your mother fills a huge pot with water. Watch her put it on the stove. Watch her turn the heat to high.

Then:

Watch your dad put raw rabbit meat into the boiling water.

Then:

Run away because all the gross things happened. Play with your brothers.

Finally:

Eat the stew at dinner. It will be stringy with half-cooked noodles. And almost tasteless. Make a face. Maybe complain.

Note on Acquisition

Rabbits should only be killed in the winter. They have disease the rest of the year. Only the healthy ones survive when the weather changes.

CHUNK RIB WITH GARLIC FOIST

CHUNK RIB WITH GARLIC FOIST

Money is incredibly problematic. I hate it, yet I think about it literally every second of every day. When I have it I feel gross. I desperately try to hold onto it. When I don't have it, I become desperate and stop sleeping. I crave structure, but a full-time job is suicide to me. I enjoy working, but I can't find a job that jibes with my temperament. My ideal job would be a ditch digger, but that job doesn't exist, the closest thing I can think of to that is gravedigger, but they use backhoes now. I would be a dishwasher which is a job that comes pretty close, but the pay is crap and the hours wouldn't allow me to pick up my daughter from school every day, which is more important than money. I can't work nights because that is when I am productive. Making art is more important than money.

I'm not making excuses as to why I can't get a job, but I am trying to explain why money is so problematic.

From the time I was 17 to the time I was 27, everything I owned, and I mean everything, could fit into a backpack. The reason for this was both practical and philosophical. I never stayed anywhere longer than a year. But then I met somebody and got married. Next thing I knew I owned a mattress. A coffee maker. More than one towel. Underwear. My name was on a lease. I had to worry about alternate side parking. I got a job. A 401k [Four Zero One K]. For three years, I was making nearly $70,000 per year. And it was brutal. I hated it. I hated it with passion. But because I was so young, and because I grew up with this belief that you can't not work, I suffered it. But the things I was working for were things I don't want. Things I don't need:

Matching plates. Two-ply toilet paper. A duvet. A duvet cover. Couches, plural. Organic coffee beans. Movie tickets. Haircuts. Rugs, plural. Bathmats, plural. Hand towels, plural. Vacations, plural. Dinner parties, plural. Night stands, plural. A subscription to *The New Yorker* [although I did get the *New York Post* delivered daily, which was pretty right on]. Parking tickets, plural. Champagne flutes, plural. Clean sheets, plural. Et al.

We struggled to have a baby. We had a baby. I quit my job. We got divorced. I became homeless. Got hit by a car. Got my shit back together with the help and kindness of my friends, especially Ramona, who let me live with her while I coalesced. Now 10 years later I still can't get back to the days of everything I own fitting in a backpack.

I have a stack of nonsense 3ft [three feet] by 7ft [seven feet] in the basement of my ex-wife's apartment. I poke around in it sometimes when I need something, but only for things I could easily get elsewhere, like computer keyboards and winter coats.

I think one of the reasons that I like living in the sublet I am living in at the moment is because me and Jonny share this ascetic notion. He holds on to very little. My girlfriend doesn't share this idea, however. She is kind of an exploding bomb of shoes and outfits and paper. But she is good looking so it is okay. Sixteen pairs of shoes though! I own one.

But let's talk about money. Two weeks ago I was living off of quarters and beans. Now I am paying rent and back rent and eating steak with money to spare. But I know it won't last. I will be homeless at the end of the month. The work will dry up. I will go back to 0 [zero]. I am okay with this.

I have this hippie friend out in California who believes the Universe will provide. But this just means she leeches from her friends. Her name is Laura. Avoid her. She will hit you up for a 20 whenever she gets a chance. And she won't pay you back. Which reminds me of a joke:

Two hippie chicks are at a farmers market in Portland, Oregon. They are standing in front of a mound of potatoes. One hippie says to the other:

"*These potatoes remind me of my boyfriends balls.*"
"*Why, because they are so big?*"
"*No, because they are so dirty.*"

Yesterday morning I had to go to the post office. I also had to go to the bank to transfer some funds. Afterward I went to the supermarket to get some stuff to make tacos. Jalapenos. Onions. Cilantro. Cheese. Corn tortillas. Limes. Tomatoes. Ground beef. Lettuce. In Worland, Wyoming, where I am from, there is a Mexican restaurant called Ranchito that makes a pretty good taco that is very American. They fry the corn tortillas in oil. It is an addition that changes the outcome. Now that I think of it, it is something my dad would do. But the tacos are simple. Fried tortillas. Ground beef. Cheese. Pico de gallo. Iceberg lettuce. Not that it's hard, but I have nailed the recipe. The trick is to not overcook the tortillas. And lots of paper towels for the grease. Vegetable oil.

While I was picking out some beef I had a thought that maybe I should do a marinade. I thought about a roast, but I didn't trust the meat. Cheap crap meat. I think you can judge meat at a market by the quality of the tomatoes that are available. The tomatoes at this place were white. Not white exactly, but not red. I had to get organic grape tomatoes. They were very red. But those were the only two options.

I ended up getting what they called a Meatloaf Mix. 1/3 ground beef. 1/3 veal. 1/3 third pork. $5.18. For nearly a pound and a half. Down and to the left they were selling ribs for $2 a pound. The ribs looked good. I got three pounds.

When I got home Tina was lying on the couch stroking her frothy mound, her big red muff glistening in the sunlight. Just jokes. When I got home Tina was working on her computer. The T on her laptop was broken so she was using an external keyboard. An external mouse. I knew she was hungry and I should have made the tacos pronto, but I really wanted to make the marinade and think about cooking the ribs. Tina ate a hank of cheese. I put *Songs:Ohia* on. [Jason Molina. Wonderful musician. Hate making a pop reference, but I am working on a biography about him, so I feel like I can bring it up without souring the moment.]

Chunk Ribs With Garlic Foist

Ingredients

3 pounds of ribs [pork or beef]
2 knobs of garlic
1/4 cup of sugar
1/4 cup of salt
A tablespoon of ground black pepper

Tools

Blender [not necessary, but see "Method" below]
Knife [very necessary, but ditto]
Rolling pin [or kitchen mallet, if you are married and have that useless shit]
Cutting board [which is useful, but not necessary]

Bowl [enough for the meat]
Baking pan [I used a pie pan and a quarter sheet pan to catch the dripping. I think I could have used a bigger pan to begin with, but I didn't, choose your own adventure.]
Tinfoil

Method

Break garlic knobs into cloves. Do this over the garbage. There will be plenty of dry skin that will be untenable. It is a frustrating task, but unavoidable. Cut tops off and peel skins. If a skin is proving to be difficult to remove, smash with the side of the knife. Big Kitchen interests tell you to do this anyway, but I think it is only necessary when you are using small amounts of garlic. Even then, though, I find it moot. Garlic can be overwhelming, and squeezing every last flavor from it is ridiculous. Unless you only have very little. But at the moment garlic is cheap. Less than $2 for six knobs. That's like 36 garlic-heavy meals.

Cut garlic cloves into chunks. Pour oil into blender. Add salt and sugar. Grind pepper on top until it seems like too much. Add more.

Blend garlic mix until smooth. Let sit.

Remove ribs from package. Place on cutting board. Rinse packaging before throwing into the garbage. This will keep the trash from smelling like rotting meat.

Cut bones from ribs. I like to have a cast iron

skillet nearly red-hot while doing this. You can fry the bone chunks and feed them to Tina. She will like them and leave you alone for a second.

Take the rolling pin and beat the ribs into ¼-inch slabs. Stack on the side of the cutting board. The meat will feel sandy as you do this. Disregard this sensation. It is just the fat flying in all directions. Don't think about it also. It is kind of gross.

Put rib chunks in bowl. Pour marinade on top. Massage into the meat. You will want to add a little cold water to the blender and put the lid back on and shake. This will get the remnants out and make you feel better. Pour on top. Massage the meat more.

Let sit for 2 hours. The ribs will come to room temperature. This will give you time to wash the dishes and clean the cutting board.

While Waiting For Garlic To Foist

Tina is hungry now. She has been eating fried ribs, which she thinks are delish, but you promised her tacos.

On a clean cutting board cut an onion into the smallest pieces you can. I like to use a pint glass of water to dip my knife in while doing this. That way the onions don't stick to the knife. Onions can be brutal on the eyes, and this helps with that. Big Kitchen recommends candles, but that is ludicrous. Even if it helps, onions are fickle, and the idea of lighting a candle to cut onions is like wearing a condom for a hand job.

Put onion pieces in a bowl. Sprinkle salt on top. Roll a lime on the cutting board [this releases the juices] and cut in half. Squeeze half over the onions and salt.

Repeat this process with the jalapenos and the tomatoes. When you get to the cilantro put a bunch, the size of a pint glass, into a pint glass. Rinse twice. Fill to the edge of the glass with cold water. Pull single stems of cilantro from the pint glass and remove the leaves. Pile the leaves on one side of the cutting board. Pile the stems on the opposite side.

When you are done, chop the leaves into coarse pieces. Put into bowl. Mix with a spoon. Let sit.

You will probably have ground beef left over from some other dinner you cooked. Fry this. Add water to soften it. Pour a ¼-cup of oil in a frying pan. Turn the heat to medium/medium high. When the oil starts shimmering test it with the edge of a corn tortilla by dipping it in. It will bubble when it is ready.

Put a mound of paper towels on a plate. Fry corn tortillas. They should bubble themselves while you are doing this. You most likely will have to flip them. Make sure to not overcook the tortillas. You can tell because they will start to harden and turn brown. Place on top of paper towels to drain.

The iceberg lettuce is simple. Remove the top

two layers of leaf. Whack the stem on something solid. Remove. Cut a hank off and put on top of the cilantro stems. Cut into pieces. Incorporate the stems.

Grate the cheese.

Take a plate from the cupboard and make a taco for your lady. Tortilla, then a spoon of beef, some cheese, a little pico de gallo, some lettuce/stem cilantro. Hand it to your lady and tell her to get lost. She will give you the stink-eye, but fuck her, that bitch is bad news.

Finalize The Rib Chunks

When the rib chunks are at room temperature, transfer them into a pie pan. Turn the oven on to 200°F. Put the pie pan on top of a quarter sheet pan to catch spillage. Cover with tinfoil.

Cook for 2 hours. The smell of garlic will overwhelm the house. While cooking write a chapter from the science fiction novel you are working on. Take ribs from the oven and put on top of the stove. Go out for the night.

The Next Morning

Turn the oven back on to 200°F. Cook for 2 more hours. The meat will disintegrate by touch. Let it sit and think of ways to use it.

My guess is that it's pretty tasty and would be good for tacos. But I also think it could be used for sandwiches. Mayonnaise, jalapenos, cilantro, and, maybe lettuce. On a roll. Maybe I will go to the deli and get a couple rolls. Lunch tomorrow.

Conclusion

Money is bunk. You think about it without knowing why. When I was younger I didn't brush my teeth sometimes because I liked smoking, I figured the film my body created that would gather on my teeth would act as a buffer that I could wash away. I can't imagine that that was true, but that was the thinking.

Being rich seems just as deplorable as being poor. The middle seems vapid. Filled with worry.

One day, and soon, housing will be a right, not a privilege, health will be a right, not a privilege, race and gender politics will be considered insane, and this age of bullying will come to an end!

Cynthia Nixon. [She eye-fucked you, Jess.] I saw her on the street the other day, with her kids. Seems legit.

New hope.

THE REMAINDERS

My daughter is in fifth grade. She is learning long division. This is an abstract concept, even for adults. But for some reason they teach this idea of the remainder. 5 goes into 14 two times with a remainder of 4. I find this absurd. It is essentially teaching our children to give up. Big Math strikes again. It's like they are saying:

"You can start this job, but you won't understand how to finish it."

Even though, in order to finish the job, you just need to keep doing the initial job the same way, over and over. Like digging for treasure, and when you get near it they stop you because they think you can't understand the gold waiting for you.

This happens later in math, too. In calculus. The derivative. But this makes sense, because it exposes the limit of the knowledge you obtain. They call it a different name: approximation. But approximation isn't a remainder.

My daughter went to a baby shower with her mom recently. There was a baby bottle filled with jelly beans. The game was to guess the amount of jelly beans. There were 814 jelly beans. George guessed 565. The winner guessed 782. That was one with a remainder of 32. The woman gave George the bottle of jelly beans. That's also a remainder.

An approximation, on the other hand, would be to measure the height and width and depth of the bottle. The height and width and depth of the bean. Knowing how big the bottle was and how big the bean was you could then approximate how many beans could possibly fit into the bottle.

I don't mean to give you a math lesson, but I do think it is important to note the difference between abstract thought and practical thought. How we learn from a very early stage to engage in this idea of giving up as a method of solving problems.

An abstract thought: I am cooking eggs for 4 people. People tend to eat 2 eggs at a time, therefore I cook 8 eggs.

A practical thought: People tend to eat 2 eggs at a time, so if I am cooking for 4 people I should cook 8 eggs. But some of those people will probably want more eggs and some will want less. I may end up with a remainder of eggs, or I may need to cook more.

An alcoholic friend of mine, used to have a catchphrase:

"I hate to see it go to waste."

He would drink the remainders of everyone's drinks. The last of any bottle of booze. Half-filled beer cans. He woke up in his car once with a pistol in the passenger seat not knowing where he was or what had happened that led to him having a pistol sitting in the passenger seat. He is sober now.

My Point Is

As Americans we are innately wasteful.

We feel guilty for eating too much. Not because we feel we are eating too much, but because we fear we are getting fat. This is a complex emotion. An emotion that should be relegated by the simple fact of just eating less, but instead becomes a tragic wasting of food.

As a dishwasher I have thrown out thousands [thousands] of pounds [pounds] of food. They are the heaviest bags. Filled with hunks of meat, cheese, bread, onions, lettuce, sauce, soups, things gross and things tasty, whole meals that could easily been packed up and brought home. This is what you should feel guilty about. Because people are starving. Not in some abstract country in Africa, or some village in South America, but here, at home, on the street corners asking for change, or standing in line, hoping to get food stamps, or the elderly choosing between medicine and eating. We all desire life. We all suffer. But nobody suffers like the starving.

Falling into poverty is grotesque. First they turn the electricity off. Which essentially makes you blind. Then the gas. You can no longer cook. Then they evict you. But because you never had any money in the first place you can't fight back. Suddenly you are on the streets. Begging for help. Or probably worse. Drugs and alcohol are a viable option. And frankly, a logical solution. Oblivion is a wonderful thing. Drunk and homeless is much better than sober and homeless. No future is better than pretending or hoping for a better future. At least you have a reason you are dying. Theoretical death is the reason the children of wealth created philosophy. Theatre. Abstract art. MFA programs. Libraries. Government. The idea of having a future.

When you are starving you have no future. There is no future. Only food. Glorious, glorious food.

Things To Save When The Lights Are Still On

Cooked meats should be put in the freezer. Things with bone, mostly. Good for stock.

Cheese rinds should be put in the freezer. Anything dairy, really. Milk, not so much, but milk goes bad pretty quick. You will know this. But certain spreadable cheeses like cream cheese and goat cheese that are starting to mold can be put in the freezer for later use, when desperate.

Vegetables should be put in the freezer. Celery, which they sell in larger chunks than can be used in a practical manner. Tomatoes. Potatoes, probably. I don't care for potatoes, so I have never done this, but otherwise they tend to sprout and wither. Pretty much any vegetable can come in handy for soups and sauces.

Anything really should be put in the freezer. Tobacco, bread, lemons, nuts. As long as the electricity is flowing you can curb the decay.

Things To Save When The Lights Go Out

Crackers. Old noodles. Oatmeal. Flours with worms [you can always sift the worms out, or not, good protein]. Pretzels. Chips. Pretty much anything dry. Just put it in a place where the mice can't get their greedy teeth on it.

Things To Save When The Gas Goes Out

At this point you are fucked. Start planning an exit strategy. You will be eating meal to meal, so make sure you have a bit of salt with you at all times. Found food tends to be a little bland. I used to take my daughter to the pools in the summer for the free lunches, and they usually sucked, but once I started bringing salt, they were pretty good. The lunch her mom would pack for her was usually pretty gourmet, so she was doing alright.

Things to Save When You Are Evicted

Food will be the last of your problems at this point. Jump in the river. Society doesn't care about you anymore. Try and eat a fish on the way down. Before you leave, take a shit in one of the closets.

How To Move Forward

If suicide doesn't fit your taste there are other options. I hear Southern California is nice all year round. Maybe move back home, that is, if you still get along with your parent/parents. You will need a bus ticket though, and unless you have the money you are kind of fucked. Nobody picks up hitchhikers anymore. Prostitution is a good way to make a few bucks. If you are really desperate, a life of crime might come in handy. Night-muggings are the best way to get a couple extra dollars without being identified. Shoplifting is pretty easy, but the more you are homeless the less likely they will let you into the shops that you can steal from, so that seems a little foolish to plan for. Age and desperation is a huge factor in this. If you are young, join a group. You will probably know which, so I won't bore you with the details. But if you are older, I would suggest sleeping on the trains for a few nights until you meet up with like-minded souls that have crash-houses and score-points to go to. I have a warning though:
Knocking the edge off is a full-time job.

Finally

Good luck and god speed. Adventure is exciting and daunting. There will be incredibly high-highs in your future, as well as low-lows. You won't know the difference in the end, but trying is the most important thing in life. Some people will disagree, and I am among them, but it's not like you have a choice. Suck it.

FREEZER SOUP

I wrote this recipe in a drunken haze late last night. Tina had returned from work. I had been writing all day. Currently we are in the act of extricating ourselves from the apartment we've been living in in Harlem. Jonny gets back soon. The freezer was full of odds and ends. Now was as good as any time to deal with these sweet morsels of gourmand-ed delights. That, plus a desire to prove a point.

I cut some sausage that Miette and Scott had made. Plus some chunks of Vermont cheddar that Miette had given me. Tina was starving and I needed her out of my business. Her critique: Yum.

This reminds me of a story my brother Luke once told me. He was moving out of an apartment and he had neglected to eat all the food in the refrigerator. He was going to be traveling by airplane, so it was impractical for him to take the food. Growing up the same way I did, he was loathe to throw the food out, which meant he would eat it before he left. It was mostly just small things, like a few olives, some hummus, chunks of fried venison, but he had purchased a large hunk of cheese without thinking. This led to him, in a very literal way, sitting down and eating the entire block of cheese. He said it was brutal. Well, his exact words were: It was a little much. But the implication was that it was brutal. Going in, and going through, and coming out.

Soups are interesting. They are kind of a one-time deal. Which, for me, makes them slightly impractical. They usually end up in the freezer. Or more likely, the trash. Then a tiny teardrop runs down my face and lands on a mound of moldy useless food warbling on top of yesterday's refuse.

With meats you can just put them in a container and let them sit. Using them whenever the mood hits. A taco. A sandwich. A nacho. Or just alone, naked and hungry at 3 [three] in the morning. A soup can't do that.

One of my favorite soups is a French Onion. It's just beef stock and onions. You are supposed to put cheese in it too, but I feel that most of the time that makes the dish overwhelming. But I also think the cheese is kind of the point in that soup, so I don't think what I am talking about is a true French Onion, semantics can suck a fatty.

Tomato soups never quite jibe, they tend to act more like sauce, and should be relegated to a can. Chicken soups can be good, but tend to be boring. Noodles and chicken are an unnatural combination when the only other ingredient is water. My daughter's mom makes a wonderful beef stew that transcends all of this, but I don't have the patience to learn it from her. There are chowders too. I have yet to garner a taste for seafood, so I will let that alone. Gumbos are the same. They include rice, which I find tricky, and almost always aren't worth the trouble. Rice is a side dish unless you know what you are doing. I don't know what I am doing. Not with rice.

Freezer Soup

My memory is a little cloudy about this, so bear with me. This recipe could easily be called: Recollection Soup. Tina claims it is one of the best things I have ever made, but I am pretty sure it can't be recreated. But I will do my best.

Ingredients

Leftover bones from a pork dish a week ago. Some meat will still be on the bone. Taste it to make sure it is not rotten.
A frozen rice and pork dish that was made and went uneaten in the freezer
A bag of frozen grapes. From your daughters lunch. Weeks old.
A few grape tomatoes in the back of the fridge
An apple in tinfoil. That Tina left behind. That I thought was an onion.
A few cloves of garlic that are growing stems
Frozen and raw white pork cutlets
Some cooked spaghetti noodles from the fridge
Some uncooked spaghetti noodles
Part of an onion
Part of a jalapeño
Half a lime
Some garlic-filled olives leftover from when your friend Jen stayed over in November. Juice included.
White bread purchased with the idea of making sandwiches that never happened
Firm tofu that might have gone bad, but was never

opened
Some butter
Lettuce. Iceberg. Some.
Water
Salt
Pepper

Tools

A pot to boil soup in. Big enough to handle all the ingredients, large enough that a hand-held mesh strainer will fit in.
 A hand-held mesh strainer
 Knife
 A frying pan
 A fork
 I feel like scissors came into use, but will remember that later. If needed.
 Cup

Method

After feeding Tina meats and cheese, fill the boiling pot with the rice thing, frozen grapes, pork bones with meat, cherry tomatoes, garlic with shoots, and olives filled with garlic with juice included. Cover with water. Set to boil.
 Next:
 Chop lettuce into small pieces. Cut other garlic into small pieces. [I learned while doing this that

if you had wet hands you can just pinch garlic to remove the skins, thereby there is no need to smash the garlic with a knife, nor a reason to peel the skins off. It is a little aggressive, but personally I get sick of fighting garlic all the time. Take back the night!] Also, add cooked spaghetti noodles and chop jalapeno.

While the soup starts to boil continue to chop lettuce and noodles and jalapeno and garlic. You will want to create a mince.

Next:

Open tofu. Cut a chunk off. Eat it. Make sure it is still good. Cut half of it into small cubes. Let sit. Cut the remainder into bigger chunks and add to soup.

Next:

Take half of the white bread from its package. Remove the crusts. Debate about what to do about them. Leave alone. Cut the crust-less bread into chunks. Take the frying pan and add any butter you have. Set heat to medium-high. Decide to add milk. Pour some milk in. Make a change of thought. Turn the oven to 400°F. You will suddenly think the soup needs to have a base of croutons on the bottom. This will take some time. Cut some more cheese and meat for Tina.

Next:

The soup will have been boiling for some time. Taste it with a spoon. I was surprised at how deep the flavor was. I hope you find that this is true for you. The rice will start acting like a jelling agent. The soup will become a gravy. Add more water.

Next:

The cutlets should be floating in a bowl of water. Thawing. I meant to mention this before. Sorry.

Next:

Take uncooked spaghetti and break in half. Put in mesh strainer. Put strainer on top of the boiling soup. Make sure the noodles are covered in liquid. Let boil with soup.

Next:

The bread mix will be ready to transfer to a baking dish [any baking dish will do, the idea is to brown the bread on all sides]. The oven should be ready. Even if it isn't, put the dish into the oven and remember that it's there.

Next:

Tina will have brought an extra stick of butter. A bottle of wine. Get her a glass of wine and put a slab of butter in the frying pan that held the bread mix. Set the burner to medium-high. When the butter melts fry the cutlets of pork. I like to dry them before hand with some paper towels, but this isn't necessary. After the first one the butter is usually starting to burn, so the idea of getting the pan back up to heat is ridiculous. If the cutlets boil, they boil. They have very little fat content anyway, so no matter what you do they will become hard and chewy.

Fry all cutlets. Put in bowl. Let sit. The small amount of juice they have will do it's best to redistribute itself. Most of it will gather on the bottom of the bowl.

Pour the pan leavings in the soup, on top of the cooking noodles.

Next:

The dish will be done when the noodles are done. Try not to overcook them. This is a matter of taste.

Next:

You will have forgotten about the croutons the way I just have. Take them out periodically from the oven. Stir. They will behave like a pudding at first. At some point they codify. Breaking into chunks. Make them as brown and hard as you can. But don't burn them.

Next:

When the croutons are done. And the noodles are done. And the soup starts to become gravy. Taste the gravy and nod to yourself. Say: Pretty tasty.

The Dish

Take a bowl. A large bowl. A soup bowl. High-sided Asian bowl. Add a couple spoonfuls of croutons to the bottom. Ladle a bit of soup on top. Add a large pinch of vegetable mince on top of that. Set aside. Cut a rested cutlet into chunks. Add on top. Add another ladle of soup. Another pinch of vegetable mince. A handful of noodles. Put a fork and spoon in it, and you are done.

Serve to Tina. She will say: Yum.

Final Thoughts

This dish could have easily backfired. It has happened before. It will again. You usually end up with a log of inedible mush. I got lucky, this time. But it is always good to try. Eating food when you are hungry is the best way to eat it. Your body wants it. No matter how you can possibly look at it, it is relative.

Joe Jr.'s has the best cheeseburger in town. I know this because of my friend James. But there is nothing specifically special about the burger. The place is nice and the people care. I am always hungry when I go there and James is a beautiful friend of mine that is wonderful company. Easy fun.

I am reading this book called *Consider the Oyster* by M.F.K. Fisher, which makes we want to eat oysters. I eat smoked oysters constantly, but oysters other ways have never appealed to me. Now they do. Particularly Oysters Rockefeller. But I will save that for another time.

Make love. Hold hands. Fight the good fight. Don't put a finger in anybody's ass unless they ask for it.

They are always asking for it.

THE PAYCHECK

THE PAYCHECK

Snow falls outside my window. Waterworks blubbers on the couch. I am gathering my thoughts. This is the last one for a while. We decided on a publication date in December. For Christmas. Something to read on the toilet while your family acts like a bunch of assholes and your body adjusts to a meal it will never be used to. You are farting and feeling bloated. Your mom is deep-throating her new boyfriend in 69 [sixty-nine] on the same bed your dad once slept in. Your sister-in-law is making jokes that nobody gets. The ham is dry, but you can't stop eating it. The shrimps remain untouched. A celebration of dirty teeth. Dirty beds. Dirty minds. Dirty smells.

But let us leave on a high note. Just two days ago I was talking to this person that was telling me:

"I mean, my girlfriend is an optimist, and I am a pessimist, it is kind of a problem."

She didn't know this was called cynicism. Not yet at least. She was only 27. She told me this more than once.

I don't mean to be cynical. I just see things. Then those things that I see get reinforced. My whole life feels like I am fighting the impulse to give up. But I don't. Not because I am strong, or because I care, but because I believe there is good in the world. I believe in my friends, and my friendships. I believe that if I love the things I love they will love me back. I think this is true 50% [fifty percent] of the time, the same way I believe that people are lying to you 50% [fifty percent] of the time. Not the worst of odds. Not the best. Half and half is good for coffee, it must be good for other things.

The paycheck changes things. It makes the weak strong. The hungry fed. The lights go back on. The gas flows like smell-less love. Suddenly, you can look your friends in the eye. Maybe buy a round. Tell a good joke. Hit on sweet babes you would love to motorboat. With their huge knockers and their New Jersey accents. Smelling like vanilla or detergent stretched out by cotton t-shirts. Nipples asunder. Braless or worse. Actually into it. Saying please no, and running back into the bathroom to do another line of cocaine.

Oh, very young, what did you leave us this time? Rhetoric. That is all.

But the paycheck changes pretty much everything.

Most of the paychecks in my life come in the form of cash. But a few, a very important few, have come in the form of a check itself. They usually included a long wait. Two weeks to two months and unless I remember wrong, they included a check-cashing place. A place to plug your nose. Only because you knew they were ripping you off, but you could walk in, give them the check and an I.D. and walk out with cash. It is so easy to take advantage of the poor.

The best one, for me, was the time I cashed a check and went to the corner of Delancey and Essex. I bought six hot dogs with everything from the hot dog cart. The idea was to share with all the six roommates in the apartment. It was so many hot dogs he put them in a bag for me. I walked proud the two blocks home. Climbed up the six flights of stairs and went inside into an empty apartment. I sat on the couch. I turned the television on. I ate all six hot dogs. I don't remember what I watched, but the hot dogs were amazing. I thought about going out to get more, but instead I fell asleep.

The usual though was when a paycheck would come in I would cash it and go and get two tacos from the fast food place. They were always the same. Flour tortilla with re-fried beans spread on top. A fried corn tortilla taco with meat and cheese and lettuce in the middle. Plus sour cream. They never disappointed.

Pizza with toppings was always an extravagance. Plain pizza was peasant food. The fancy ones were for the rich guys. There was a certain slice that had ground beef and American cheese that was kind of the ultimate. The crust was thick and crunchy, like Chicago-style. It stuck to the top of your mouth. The problem with it though, was that it took so long to cook you would find yourself pacing while waiting for it. Luckily you had to pay first, otherwise they would have thrown your ass to the curb.

There was a place on Colfax in Denver, near High Street that sold a wonderful burger. The hours were sketchy, but if you caught it right, damn!

Also, on Colfax, a place called Pete's that had a gyro that was incredible.

The place in Powell, Wyoming, that had the best biscuits and gravy.

That taco stand outside the hotel in Mexico during spring break. So much anger. An angry taco. But they liked me and Johnny Bush because we wore pants. Jeans even.

Philadelphia, naturally, a cheese steak, from a street cart. And afterwards Jacob catching a gnarly toke from a random dog on the corner. My 21st birthday.

Things my brother Buck does.

Things my brother Charley does.

Things my brother Luke does.

Things my brother Jade does.

No offense, Mom, but force a guy to learn to cook, he will never be a bridesmaid.

Final, Finale

Food can be tasty even if you are poor. Being poor is a full-time job. Everybody needs love.

ONE MORE FOR
THE ROAD

Nothing ever happens soon enough. Then suddenly, there is never enough time. You know? The old, same old. The echo chamber. Plenty of time, but no money. Plenty of money, but no time. The curse of the working class. That's not true. The curse of the working class is that you have to devote your existence to somebody else in order to survive. Liberal feudalism. That's how they built the pyramids.

But time is money, right? We should all be rich until we die, right? What, with all that time that we have on our hands. Just waiting. Waiting and waiting. Waiting for death. And then we have an infinite amount of time to waste! This thought is not profound. Nor ironic. Idiotic maybe. Think all the thoughts you want, it all ends the same way. Blackness. Cold, irrefutable blackness.

But casualty is fun. Knowing there is an end gives purpose to things that didn't have purpose before. Like wills. My guess is that rich people get off while writing their wills. The dominant vulture choosing who can and can't eat from the rotting corpse that really doesn't, and never did, belong to them.

The self-made man is a myth. Albert Einstein is literally the only one I can think of. And really, had he not come along when he did, he would have just as easily dissolved into the miasma of current trends that almost all original thinkers do. Denied. Ignored. Untenable.

A place without money.

But Einstein, he was good. When he got married, after the marriage, he took his wife home. He couldn't open the door because he lost the key. They had to get a locksmith.

I am terrified of being locked out.

I hold my keys in my hand as I close the door. Just to make sure I have them. Because of Einstein. Just jokes. He is pretty good, but I only think of him in an abstract way. Although, there is that story about him giving a cigar to that other guy and it's gross so the guy drops it into the river "on accident."

But Jonny is on a plane. Coming back from Southeast Asia. Me and Tina have been blowing out for over a week now. Tina has a few things. A bird. A fish. I have a plant I have been nurturing since about 10 years ago. There are some shoes. A bag or two of clothes. Some other bags of paper. Books. Food things. Vibrators. Pillows. Dead birds. Queso. A fish.

I don't know. It has been quite a few days of cleaning. Packing. Throwing. Things out. The old, get lost. I am coming home. Get going for now. Come back in the fall.

Tina got in the car. We borrowed the car. From a friend. The bird and the plant and the fish, were sitting shotgun. Heading to Brooklyn. I said goodbye. I went back up to clean.

I have been cleaning for hours now. But I left something in the fridge that I thought would be useful today, but was not, but was some food that was tasty. It was supposed to be eaten last night, but Tina got some Chinese food on her way home from work. When she got home she said:

"You know why I like Chinese food? Because it is low-mein-tanence."

I laughed at her joke. Then we ate the food. It was tasty. She packed for a while. Then she went to bed. I stayed up. Nothing else happened.

In the morning we took the train downtown. We got the car. It was raining. We pulled over and got egg sandwiches. They were tasty. When we were pulling out onto the street, a woman whacked on the back of the car. She went over to Tina's side. Tina rolled the window down. The woman yelled at her. She was a jerk. We were near a hospital. It was raining.

But the food that was left behind. I got to get out of here.

Tacos for Jonny

Ingredients

4 lean pork steaks left in the fridge before moving
A small amount of cheese left over from the hunk that
Miette gave you
A small amount of onion
The best parts of an iceberg lettuce that will most likely
go into the trash
Butter
Salt

Tools

Frying Pan
Fork
Bowl

Method

Put frying pan on medium heat. Add butter. Wait until it turns brown. Add pork steaks. One at a time. Two if the pan is large. Fry on both sides. Put in bowl. Salt.

Let sit.

Cut cheese and onion into small chunks. Add to each other. Put in container. Put container in fridge.

Find the best leaves that belong to the iceberg lettuce. Peel off. Cut into chunks. Put in container. Put container in fridge.

Take pork steaks from bowl. Cut into strips. Fry

again in frying pan. Transfer to container. Pour juice from frying pan on top. Put lid on container. Put container in fridge.

The Dish

I don't even know. Jonny will be coming home from a 24-hour flight. I doubt he will be hungry. But, maybe. There are flour tortillas in the fridge. Also, some wine and some vodka. If I were you, I would just drink all the booze and try to get some sleep. Maybe drink some water every couple hours when you wake up.

But if you are hungry, heat up the pork in a frying pan. Take the pan from the flame and use the flame to heat the tortillas. Add some cheese/onion mix on top. Maybe some hot sauce? Add lettuce. Enjoy.

ABOUT THE AUTHOR

Joey Truman is a writer and artist based in New York City. He performs with the bands UM, Escalators, and Soft Inserts. His upcoming books from Whisk(e)y Tit press include *CockKnocker,* a mystery novel, and *Ruiner,* a book about bees. And forthcoming from Ugly Duckling Presse, *BIOGRAPH>LAST YEAR WAS PRETTY//SHITTY.*

ABOUT THE PUBLISHER

Whisk(e)y Tit is committed to restoring degradation and degeneracy to the literary arts. We work with authors who are unwilling to sacrifice intellectual rigor, unrelenting playfulness, and visual beauty in our literary pursuits, often leading to texts that would otherwise be abandoned in today's largely homogenized literary landscape. In a world governed by idiocy, our commitment to these principles is an act of civil service and civil disobedience alike.

ACKNOWLEDGEMENTS

Tina Satter
Miete Gillette
Murphey Wilkins
James Oseland
Jack Warren
Scott Halvorsen Gillette
Peanut Gallery
George Truman
Margaret Sloan
Jess Barbagallo
Jonathan Butterick